the Holy Land

A GUIDE

W. Joseph Clark

Our Sunday Visitor Publishing Division
Our Sunday Visitor, Inc.
Huntington, Indiana 46750

Copyright © 1986 by W. Joseph Clark

Write:
Our Sunday Visitor Publishing Division
Our Sunday Visitor, Inc.
200 Noll Plaza
Huntington, Indiana 46750

Library of Congress Catalog Card Number: 86-61593
International Standard Book Number: 0-87973-546-5

Cover design by James E. McIlrath

Printed in the United States of America

*Dedicated to the Franciscan
Fathers of the Holy Land,
Custodians of the Holy Places*

Contents

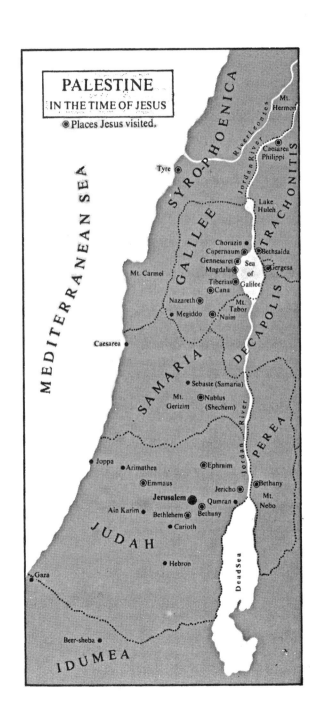

PALESTINE
IN THE TIME OF JESUS

◎ Places Jesus visited.

1

Ave Maria •
Nazareth: Basilica of the Annunciation

"AVE MARIA" was the first greeting of Christianity. The Annunciation was the first event of the Christian Era. Everything that happened before that was prophecy — promises that the Messiah would come. But with the Angel Gabriel's awesome salutation to Mary, the world was assured that the fact of salvation was at hand, that a new day was dawning for humanity.

It is appropriate to begin our pilgrimage at the Basilica of the Annunciation in the Galilean town of Nazareth, the traditional site where the Angel told Mary that she was to bear a Child who was to be called Jesus. The basilica is a majestic building of white limestone. Its brilliance is dazzling in the Holy Land's intense sun.

This shrine is located on Casa Nova Street, two short blocks up a slight hill from Nazareth's main thoroughfare — Pope Paul VI Street. Standing before the basilica, we immediately note its unusual architecture, its oriental flavor, and the great octagonal cupola rising above the roof. The face of the building is decorated with reliefs of the Annunciation, and larger-than-life images of the Gospel writers — Saints Matthew, Mark, Luke, and John.

Latin inscriptions are chiseled into the face of this church, inscriptions which are also chiseled into the memories of Catholics around the world: *ANGELUS DOMINI NUNTIAVIT MARIAE — VERBUM CARO FACTUM EST ET HABITAVIT IN NOBIS* — "The Angel of the Lord spoke to Mary — And the Word was made flesh and dwelt among us."

The Annunciation was a glorious blessing to Mary, and to all mankind. And to help us better understand the shrine that commemorates that great event, we have the benefit of our own blessing. He is Father Gumbert Ludwig, O.F.M., a Franciscan priest assigned to the Basilica of the Annunciation.

"Welcome! Welcome, my friend!' he says, with his hand outstretched and a matter-of-fact warmth in his eyes. Father Gumbert is a veteran priest who has many years of hard work to his credit — eighteen years in China "until the communists forced us out," a quarter century in Egypt, and now five years in Nazareth. He is a scholar with callused hands. His silver-gray hair is closely cropped, and he is comfortable in his order's austere brown robes and simple sandals. He is a direct man, with a firm handshake.

"First, it is important to understand the background of this church in order to appreciate it," the German-born priest tells us. "Come, follow me!" The Franciscan steps around to the left side of the church and, producing a ring of keys, unlocks a black iron gate, which swings on rusted hinges. A few steps beyond the gate, and around a corner, we come upon an archaeological site.

"Here, this is a typical home of Nazareth at the time Mary and Joseph were living here," he declares. "You see these levels?" His right hand gestures expressively toward the site. There is one space, a rough oval, about fifteen feet across at its widest point. This is a floor area, set about a foot below ground level. Beyond is a second floor, somewhat smaller in area, and set down a few steps lower than the first.

"This first level was the living area — not very large at all — and it was here that a family ate and slept and received guests," the priest explains. "There was very little furniture. No beds or chairs. People ate and slept upon simple mats made of woven palm fronds. Perhaps someone with some wealth had sheepskins, or a table, but most people lived very simply.

"Next, you go down to the lower level," he continues, gesturing to the storage room carved into the Nazareth bedrock. "This was a pantry of sorts. Here, look at the holes cut into the rock floor. These were storage silos for keeping grain, and perhaps olives, or dates, or wine. Because of all these silos cut into the stone floor, we believe this area couldn't have been used for living space. Imagine an infant toddling here. It would be very dangerous. He'd surely fall into one of the storage silos. So, we're certain that nearly all the living was done in the single upper room."

Father Gumbert now points out a blackened recess in the stone wall. "That was an oven," he says, "cut right into the wall. Limestone here is quite soft and can be cut away without much difficulty, and nearly every home had an oven like this one. Everyone baked their own bread. Mary certainly baked bread for the Holy Family. And it wasn't so difficult. First a wood fire was set in the oven, and this heated all the stones. When the fire burnt down to embers and coals, they were swept out and the dough was placed into the preheated stone oven to bake. Quite simple!"

Father Gumbert is one of the many Franciscan priests working in the Holy Land who have developed intense fascinations with archaeology. Each one of them, in addition to his religious and social duties, busies himself with a careful study of the Church's past. Their work over the recent decades has unearthed physical links to the Gospels. Their labors are producing physical proofs of the truthful basis of Christian traditions.

"Ah, ha! Come look at this!" the enthusiastic priest exclaims, springing from one stone to another — and off we go to inspect another fragment, another shred of evidence which, when joined to all the other finds, presents a beautiful mosaic of history and a unique perspective of the early Church — a perspective which, until very recently, lay buried in the silt and rubble of generations.

Archaeologists have traced human settlement in Nazareth back to the Middle Bronze Age, about 2000 B.C. More evidence confirms that it was a modest community a thousand years later, when King David ruled in Jerusalem — twenty-eight generations before the birth of Jesus. At the time of the Annunciation, Nazareth was a small crossroads community in the Roman province of Galilee. And all through this ancient history, available evidence indicates it was a relatively poor town, with a subsistence economy based on simple agriculture.

Another small house, similar to the one Father Gumbert described, stands beneath the great cupola of the basilica. But this house has one very important difference. Christian traditions, dating back to the early Church, associate this house with the Annunciation. It is called the Grotto of the Annunciation, a typical home of Nazareth, about eighteen feet across and nine feet from floor to ceiling. Father Gumbert claims that if one looks beneath the altar, and the religious articles, and the cascades of colorful, fresh flowers, one will find a home very much like the one at the archaeological site outside the church — simple, efficient, and typically Nazareth.

Pilgrims are usually so anxious to visit the Grotto that they tend to ignore the great shrine built above it. This is one of the newest churches in the Holy Land, and its unusual architecture reflects the great efforts made to protect and cherish the holy site within. The design as well as construction was difficult also because of the great number of archaeologically significant sites crisscrossing its lot.

Back in the 1950s when the Franciscans decided to build the basilica, they worked with architect G. Muzio and Israel's largest building firm, Solel Boneh, which incidentally is a cooperative owned by the Histadrut — the national labor union. Together they tackled the formidable project.

We start our visit on the spiral stone steps just inside the front doors. Ascending, we pass a series of beautiful stained-glass windows illuminating the way with brilliant color and, at the top, enter the upper church. This is a very spacious room, light and airy. Permanent seating is in place, for this area serves as the parish church for Nazareth's four thousand Roman Catholics. On the front wall is an enormous mosaic — fifteen hundred square feet — depicting Jesus and St. Peter standing on Mount Zion.

The giant cupola towers nearly two hundred feet overhead. It is designed as a great inverted lily. "Its roots are in heaven," Father Gumbert explains, and it "pours out fragrance and light upon the earth." Look closely at the petals of this extraordinary lily, and you'll see that they are all shaped to form the letter "M" — for Mary.

You can't stand directly beneath the cupola because there's no floor there. Instead, there's a railing to protect one from stumbling off the edge and down to the lower church. Directly beneath the great cupola, down in the foundations of the basilica, is the site of the Annunciation — and there is nothing between it and the heavens except for the great inverted lily.

Before returning downstairs, we'll look around the upper church and admire the many beautiful art pieces. The walls are lined with pictures of our Lady, each from a different country and a different culture. One is struck by the thought that Catholics around the world think of Mary as being one of "their own," that they fashion *her* image as part of *their* cultures.

Here is a statue of Mary with the Infant Jesus sitting on the throne of the dragon, surely a gift of Taiwan's Catholics. But if you're not certain, that Taiwanese flag on the globe in the Infant's hand will confirm any suspicion. Canada's Madonna, appropriately, rules over forests and lakes. India's Madonna is dressed in a sari, and her eyes are beautifully almond. The Catholics of the United States contributed a spectacular silver Madonna, inspired by Chapter 12 of the Book of Revelation: ". . .a woman clothed with the sun, with the moon under her feet, and on her head a crown of twelve stars." Dozens of other likenesses of Mary line the walls and reveal the many visions of our Lady which are seen by Catholics of every continent.

Returning downstairs, we enter the lower church, which is darker, cooler, and set in abstract designs. Contrasting marble in the floors form jagged, flashing patterns. Concrete beams overhead form rigid, radiating perspectives. And intense colors in the abstract stained-glass windows cast very strong hues of red and yellow into the church. One has the sensation of walking through a science-fiction scene, an architecture of another time, another place. Yet, there is still a very strong religious atmosphere, the scent of incense, the image of the cross.

In the center of the lower church is a sunken area, square and about thirty feet across. At the rear of this square is the Grotto of the Annunciation.

In the center of the square, there is an altar. For Mass, people gather around the upper edges of this sunken square and stand behind a protective railing. It's an unusual perspective — looking down toward the priests celebrating Mass — but then, this is a very unusual church.

When we enter, a group of Japanese pilgrims are gathered in that sunken square in front of the Grotto. They are praying in Japanese, and, although we don't understand the words, the cadence of their phrases is familiar to every Catholic. The mere rhythms of their words tell us they are praying, "Hail Mary . . . full of grace . . . the Lord is with thee. . . ."

We stand in the shadows and watch as their priest leads them to the Grotto, and each pilgrim glimpses within, commits the sight and its feelings to memory, and offers a brief prayer. Two young women, perhaps in their twenties, kneel before the Grotto and remain there in prayer for several minutes after the rest of their group have filed back up to the main floor.

A group of French pilgrims at the railing stand respectfully quiet while the two women finish their prayers, bless themselves, and hurry back to their group. The French Catholics then descend to the sunken square and, with their priest leading, begin singing "Ave Maria" in Latin. They start quietly, with hushed words and melodies. But their intensity begins to grow until the volume of their hymn fills the church. It echoes aloft and reverberates through that great inverted lily suspended from the heavens. Their singing seems to penetrate all the rocks and concrete, as indeed it penetrates my body. I shiver, feeling goose bumps rise across the back of my neck while I listen to their beautiful voices.

And so throughout the day, a steady stream of pilgrims flows through this church. Some come in organized groups, some with only a couple of friends, and some come alone. Several pilgrims wander through rather quickly, and I think this is a shame. They have not had time to savor the greatness of this church.

Some of the more successful pilgrim groups are those organized within parish churches and traveling with a priest. These groups usually travel by commercial tour-group buses, and the priest and the tour operator negotiate the specific desires of the group, so nobody feels rushed and the pilgrimage progresses at a satisfactory rate.

Those who travel alone, or with a small, private group, have the most flexibility. And often they are the ones who spend the most time at particular shrines. One day, at the Basilica of the Annunciation, I noticed an elderly couple seated together on the steps leading to the Grotto of the Annunciation. It was late morning. Pilgrim groups came and went, each filing past them on the stairs. And yet they stayed in place. The old fellow would alternate between staring into the Grotto and reading from the Gospels. The woman beside him seemed more lost in her thoughts, staring blindly and smiling, as if delighting in some inner joy. They remained there for hours.

"The Grotto has been associated with the Annunciation since the earliest days of the Church," Father Gumbert says. "The people of Nazareth followed Jesus, and they recognized the site of the Annunciation as a sacred area. They worshiped here, and we have much evidence of this."

The Franciscan says that sometime around A.D. 60, Roman soldiers apparently helped restore the Grotto, which was then in use by the local Christian community. But, as years passed, the tiny Grotto proved too small, so a church was built incorporating it into a larger building. This church followed the design of Jewish synagogues of the region and was built sometime around A.D. 200. One of the stones of this church has the Greek inscription "XE MAPIA" — "Hail Mary." "This tells us that Mary was venerated long before the Council of Ephesus in 431," Father Gumbert notes.

Various elements of this ancient synagogue-church have been discovered, and part of its south wall is now incorporated into the sunken square of the lower church. Other inscriptions were found on the walls of this ancient building, and Father Gumbert translates a few. "I made here the veneration of light; Lord Christ, save your servant Valerian. . . . Pray for one fallen for Christ," says one of the inscriptions, and the Franciscan speculates that the "one fallen for Christ" might have been Conon, who was martyred in the year 248 and who, before dying, claimed, "I come from Nazareth, I am a relative of Jesus, and I worship him as did my ancestors."

An interesting bit of graffiti found on these walls was dated to about A.D. 246 and says, "Venerate a Roman Emperor? Me? I am a Nazarene." Surely, this early Christian was downright indignant over any suggestion he join pagan practices.

With the conversion of the Roman Empire to Christianity, a great building boom was experienced in the Holy Land, and sometime around the year 400 a Byzantine basilica was built above the Grotto. Most of the older synagogue-church was destroyed to make way for the new basilica, and skilled archaeologists today are able to decipher where the foundation of one begins and the other ends. There are many remnants of this ancient basilica to be seen today at the shrine — parts of walls, the remains of a nave, fragments of mosaics and frescoes that decorated the church. At one point, Franciscan scholars were able to distinguish six layers of paint on parts of the Byzantine basilica's stone wall, and each layer revealed a different design and color, including paintings of flowers, garlands, and Christian symbols. Some scholars believe that at this time the Grotto of the Annunciation served as the basilica's baptistry.

With the Saracen Arab invasions of A.D. 640, the basilica was damaged and suffered subsequent decline until the Crusades; but then, in 1100, Tancred de Hauteville built a new church on the site. This must have been a marvelous building, as we can see from the remains of columns and walls

The Holy Land

which have been identified. Lovely as it was, the Crusader church stoodonly until the year 1263, when it was demolished during the Muslim reconquest of the Holy Land.

An endearing legend developed from this battle. It claims that when all seemed lost, and Arab hordes were just about to overwhelm the Crusader defenders, a company of angels appeared and lifted the church from its foundations. The building was then carried to safety, far across the sea. And if you visit the village of Loretto, also known as the Nazareth of Italy, you will be shown the "Santa Casa" which angels delivered there so long ago.

It is a tribute to Catholic persistence that in 1730, when the Holy Land was a backwater province of the Turkish Ottoman Empire, the Franciscans returned again to this holy site and built a new church. That church remained to serve Nazareth's Catholics until 1955, when it was torn down to make way for the new basilica.

Thus, the present basilica is the fifth church to stand on this site. Completed in 1969, the Basilica of the Annunciation is a monument to both Catholic devotion to sites made holy by the events of the Gospels, and to the very rich history which followed.

"Actually, Franciscans were here for more than a century before they built the 1730 church," Father Gumbert said. "Our records show that Franciscans were here in 1620, but the Muslim rulers would not allow them to build a church. At best, they could simply live among the ruins. And so they stayed with those ruins for more than a century, in the summer heat and winter rains, without a roof, until finally they were granted permission to build their church."

The abundant history of this holy site still continues. One sees recent works of art added to the church — a panoramic landscape of Pope Paul VI's historic pilgrimage to the Holy Land, a new Madonna set into the walls, a touching mosaic presented on behalf of refugees. This last work was a thankful inscription at the bottom: "In gratitude from thousands of Polish children delivered from Russian slavery and Nazi oppression. In the Holy Land and the Free World they found a home."

Those children are now adults, and some of them are today Israeli Catholics, members of the Nazareth parish. They are part of a very rich and varied Catholic community in this Galilean town — a community as old as those first "Nazarenes" who followed Jesus during His ministry on earth, as new as the pilgrims who have stepped into the Basilica of the Annunciation for the first time in their lives while you were reading this chapter.

Those newcomers are of special importance to Father Gumbert. He likes to stand by the gates of the basilica and greet visitors, drawing them into the experience of being part of Nazareth and the continuing heritage that started at the Annunciation. For him, the regular parish members — his "flock" — are a stable group and need only a modest amount of tending.

Following the example of the Good Shepherd, Father Gumbert keeps watch for strays, using his best talents to bring them back to the flock. And often these strays are found among pilgrims.

"A pilgrimage," he tells us, "is not just for the devout. It's also very important for doubters. Surely, every day we see groups of devout Catholics coming here, but we also see people who are just curious about the Holy Land. There is something inside them that pushes them to come home. They want to see, to feel, to touch something. They are not sure what it is, but there is a motivation for searching. They want to find something. Maybe they are simply looking for themselves, or maybe they are looking for their faith — sometimes these two things are the same thing, they can come together.

"For devout Catholics, there is no problem," he goes on. "They have a good idea of what they want from a pilgrimage. And if they can't find what they are looking for, they ask and they receive. And sometimes they ask difficult questions, and sometimes we surprise them. A while ago, a group of Chinese Catholics wanted to hear Mass in the basilica. And they were quite surprised to learn that I was capable of offering Mass in Chinese.

"The seeker is a different person," the Franciscan notes, "because what he wants is not always clear to him. He must be helped along that difficult path."

Besides the pilgrims and parishioners, the eight priests and four brothers working at the basilica are also very much concerned over the Grotto of the Annunciation. "Its stones have been weakened. It is not very strong," Father Gumbert points out. Centuries of often-violent history have damaged the holy site and now threaten its future.

Today, an artistic iron gate protects the Grotto from the thousands of visitors who constantly flow through the basilica. It is obvious that many of those visitors only want to touch those ancient stones which were part of sacred events — but even this is prohibited. At best, most pilgrims can only gaze into the Grotto but cannot enter. They can peer through the iron gate and bring an image of the Annunciation to their minds and hearts.

There is discussion now of hermetically sealing the Grotto, but there is some debate over this. Sealing the holy site, even behind clear glass, would surely preserve it for future centuries — but it would also create a serious barrier. Hermetic sealing — an air-tight encasement — would also create a psychological barrier for some people. Many pilgrims want an intimate feeling of actual contact with holy sites. For them, it is very important to walk the same streets that Jesus walked, and to drink from the same wells, and to touch the same stones.

For others, however, this is not particularly important. Many Catholics are capable of making spiritual pilgrimages. They are capable of traveling halfway across the world within their own thoughts. For them, it is important to know that the Grotto of the Annunciation does exist and responsible Catholic authorities are taking care of it.

Regardless of the outcome — whether the Grotto is hermetically sealed or repaired by modern, "unseen" techniques, or traditional craftsmen are called in for conventional restoration work — Catholics can be assured that the Grotto is receiving very careful professional attention. And this is a relatively recent benefit. One need think back only a couple of centuries to a time when Catholics were prohibited from mending a single stone of the Grotto.

We now leave the basilica, knowing that it and its precious Grotto are in competent and loving hands. We turn southward, toward a little village in the Judean hills called Ain Karem, and from there to another small town — Bethlehem. Only after visiting these holy places will we return to Nazareth and try to view it from another perspective — as the "hometown" of the Holy Family, as a community where the youthful Jesus grew and started His ministry.

2 *Magnificat* •
Ain Karem: Shrine of the Visitation

ST. LUKE tells us that after the Annunciation, Mary traveled "as quickly as she could to a town in the hill country of Judah" to visit with her older cousin, Elizabeth. That town, Christian scholars agree, is the community of Ain Karem, a picturesque cluster of stone buildings just five miles west of the center of Jerusalem.

Today, Ain Karem is incorporated into the municipal boundaries of the Israeli capital, but nevertheless, a relative isolation enables this lovely village to maintain a very distinct charm and identity. It is located deep in a green and sheltered valley, and the access road is steep and serpentine.

The town takes its name from a cool, clear spring there, which gurgles from the bedrock and then trickles down to irrigate vineyards and orchards planted in the valley. *Ain* in Hebrew is the word for spring. *Karem* means vineyard. That spring still flows, just as it did twenty centuries ago, and it waters grapevines, olive and apricot orchards, and tracts of pine forest lining its route.

It was here that a joyous Mary embraced her cousin and then offered one of the most poetic and devotional prayers of the Christian heritage — The Magnificat:

"My soul magnifies the Lord,
and my spirit rejoices in God my Savior;
for he has regarded the lowly state of his handmaiden.
For behold, henceforth all generations will
call me blessed;
for he who is mighty has done great things for me.
and holy is his name,
and his mercy is on those who fear him,
from generation to generation." (Lk 1:46-50)

People who visit the Shrine of the Visitation at Ain Karem today will find this beautiful prayer fired into ceramic tile on a great wall in the courtyard. The prayer can be read in English. It can also be found in Latin, and in French and Spanish and Hebrew and Arabic, and indeed in nearly one hundred languages.

Bible students may recall a time in remote antiquity when pagan peoples of Mesopotamia were so audacious and sacrilegious that they began to build a tower which they could use to invade heaven. The Almighty was angered by this shamelessness, and confused the builders by causing each to speak a different language. Unable to communicate, the building project stopped and the people scattered across the earth. The land was called Babel, later Babylon.

Standing before this beautiful wall at Ain Karem, one sees a moving expression of penitence. Humanity was punished with many languages because it tried to create its own way to heaven. But a later artist, in an inspired act, took those numerous and confused languages of punishment and used them to inscribe echoes of the sole legitimate path to redemption — devotion to God. And that is precisely what the Magnificat is: a beautifully composed, melodic expression of devotion to God.

That joyful meeting of Mary and Elizabeth produced another very memorable phrase. Elizabeth knew Mary was carrying an Infant and, in greeting her, exclaimed, "Of all women you are the most blessed, and blessed is the fruit of your womb" — and we recite these words of happiness each time we pray the Hail Mary.

But Mary's purpose in visiting her cousin in Ain Karem was not merely to be showered with accolades and praise. Mary, though carrying a Child herself, came to work. She came to help Elizabeth, who was many years her senior and then in the sixth month of pregnancy. Elizabeth was to become the mother of St. John the Baptist, a man who, in his own compelling way, was to "proclaim the greatness of the Lord."

Mary lived three months at Ain Karem, and must have developed a familiar feeling for this hilly landscape and bucolic village. How many times did she hike to the clear spring to fetch water for the house's drinking needs, washing, cooking, and laundry? How many times did she climb the steep hill — more than six hundred fifty feet vertical, taller than most "skyscraper" buildings — just east of Ain Karem? For she must have climbed this formidable hill every time she walked into Jerusalem, where her own parents lived.

The Shrine of the Visitation is itself a collection of structures, built one upon another over the centuries in an appealing way, even if the architecture is not particularly unified. Deep within the shrine, at the lowest level, is a crypt which commemorates the home of Elizabeth and her husband, Zechariah.

Christians have been conducting religious services here for at least sixteen centuries, when Byzantine rule finally made Christian public worship possible. Before this, however, it is likely that the crypt was the site of secret Christian services, conducted in defiance of pagan Roman edicts. Indeed, this site is identified in some very ancient writings, such as the Protevangelium of James — written a mere century after the Crucifixion, and certainly within a time frame during which oral traditions remain accurate. The Protevangelium, incidentally, is part of records known as "pseudepigrapha," writings which the Church considers useful historical documents, although they are not canonical, or written under divine inspiration. Much of early Church history depends on such pseudepigrapha, since canonical writings such as the Gospels are concerned more with inspired religious teachings than with technical descriptions of places and history.

It is cool and damp in the crypt. But one cannot help but imagine that it was much different twenty centuries ago when Mary visited her cousin here. Since then, devout Christians have built church upon basilica upon shrine over this site, and somehow all the construction seems to have obscured some of the rustic character of the original dwelling. This problem is not noticed at the Basilica of the Annunciation because of the sharp distinction between the church and the crypt. But here in Ain Karem the situation is quite different, and distinctions between the church and the venerated site are less clear.

Thus, after viewing the crypt, it is useful to step outdoors for a while, and to find a shady spot with a view of the valley. Sitting here, with a bit of imagination and some common sense, might help us envision what this village was like during the summer before the birth of Jesus.

Certainly the shapes of the hills and valley were virtually the same. Now, as then, drought-resistant evergreens grow on the higher slopes, while the lower land is planted with vines and fruit trees. The lower land has richer soil and more water. The village of Ain Karem was most likely in the same location, clustered near the place where the spring emerges from the limestone bedrock. Here the water is cleanest and best for drinking. Further along, the stream is a bit more soiled and better used for irrigating crops.

The houses were then, as now, built of blocks of limestone. This is the most common building material available, and it's soft enough to be easily shaped with hammer and chisel. Although some evergreens grow in the region, the quality of their timber is not very good; stone is both cheaper and stronger. Most of the houses are oriented toward the center of the valley, and there are many gardens and unpaved streets.

Ain Karem is a friendly village, populated today by a mixed community of Christian Arabs and Israeli Jews. There are several artists and craftsmen living here. They have studios here and a few galleries, but they usually give their works to the commercial galleries and hotels in the city for sale. Ain Karem is informal. Children run barefoot on the street. Old men sit together on simple chairs, shaded from the bright sun by the intricate latticework of grape arbors. And here they sip thick coffee and discuss politics, the weather, the price of eggs, and other matters of great importance.

You can hear the braying of donkeys and the music of songbirds here, and the prevailing west breeze carries with it the fragrances of the pine forests. There seems to be much laundry hanging on clotheslines.

There was probably much laundry back in the days of Elizabeth and Zechariah too. St. Luke tells us that Zechariah was an important priest at the Temple of Jerusalem, indeed so important that he was one of the few who entered the Most Holy Place to tend its altar. Elizabeth was a direct descendant of Aaron, the brother of Moses, and first high priest of Israel. "And they were both righteous before God," St. Luke tells us, "walking in all the commandments and ordinances of the Lord blameless" (Lk 1:6).

At first we might think that Elizabeth and Zechariah were devout, honest, charitable people, and certainly this must be true.

But St. Luke also tells us that they scrupulously observed the "ordinananances" of the Lord. And this meant they kept a *kosher* house — ritually clean. Also, Zechariah's duties at the Temple required immaculately clean vestments. Clotheslines were certainly a common site in Ain Karem during those days, too.

How might we picture daily life during Mary's visit at Ain Karem? Surely Elizabeth, being aged and in her last three months of pregnancy, was virtually restricted to bed or an easy chair. And since Zechariah had his priestly duties, nearly all the household work likely fell to Mary. It was likely that Mary did most of that laundry and walked to market each day, cut salads, baked bread, and tended to many other chores.

But Mary was here during the late spring and summer — pleasant months which, in this part of the world, mean warm temperatures and not a single drop of rain. And at the end of Elizabeth's term, St. John was born and Mary returned home to Nazareth.

The following six months in Ain Karem must have been a time of increasing difficulty and danger. First, when Mary left, Elizabeth must have had more work to do, besides caring for the infant. Autumn brought cooling days, and then the rains. Zechariah's way up the steep hill toward his work at the Temple of Jerusalem must have been treacherous. And being a priest at the Temple was even more dangerous — for these were the most outrageous days of the dying and mad King Herod.

In the winter, after the birth of Jesus, the Holy Family fled to Egypt. But Elizabeth, Zechariah, and John remained behind — and John was but an infant, condemned, subject to Herod's edict that all infants under age two should be slaughtered. The infant St. John was at great risk of becoming one of the martyred Holy Innocents, especially since his father was a well-respected priest and the birth to aged parents was considered as an extraordinary blessing. It would be difficult to hide this child.

Yet the babe was hidden, and pilgrims touring the Shrine of the Visitation can see the place where tradition says he was secluded while squads of Roman soldiers went on their bloody rampage.

About this time, the insane Herod ordered yet another outrage which must have sent shivers of fear through Ain Karem. The king suspected that he was dying, and that when he passed there would be great joy in the land. But he was determined to prevent his funeral from becoming a national celebration among the Jews. To turn his death into a true day of mourning, Herod ordered the imprisonment of scores of prominent scholars, wise men, and priests. When he died, all of these dignitaries were to be butchered immediately.

Was Zechariah prominent enough to be arrested and condemned by Herod? History is silent on this point. But we can be sure that, at the very least, he was in great fear of being included among these hostages.

It should be noted that when Herod did die, his sister Salome kept the event secret for a while — just long enough for her to move effectively to free the hostages. And the mad King Herod's death then became a double celebration in Jerusalem.

Then, times took a turn for the better, and, according to St. Luke, the young St. John "grew and became strong in spirit." It is also written in this Gospel that during these younger years St. John "was in the wilderness" (Lk 1:80). We can see at least part of that wilderness from the lovely plazas outside the shrine. We can see the rolling Judean hills, which were home to many great men before St. John walked upon them. The Patriarch Abraham walked here, and Isaac and Jacob. Joshua reclaimed these hills as part of the Promised Land. Young David followed his sheep here, and in the Valley of Elah, where these hills roll out to the coastal plain, his faith was his only shield in his battle with Goliath, the Philistine giant. One can walk due west from Ain Karem, following the same valley for about fifteen miles, and come to the village of Eshtaol, the home of the mighty Samson.

St. John, having a priest as his father and a direct descendant of Aaron as his mother, must have been very familiar with all those great people of this land's history. And then came his turn for greatness. He walked through the wilderness proclaiming, "I baptize you with water, but he who is mightier than I is coming, the thong of whose sandals I am not worthy to untie; he will baptize you with the Holy Spirit and with fire" (Lk 3:16).

Such thoughts can wander through a pilgrim's mind while he wanders through the labyrinthine Shrine of the Visitation. But be careful not to get lost! It's quite easy to be stepping from a Byzantine passage and enter a church built above a grotto. Turn to one side and there's a modern chapel with classical lines. Turn around, and you'll face the apse of a Crusader church built eight centuries ago.

The art at this shrine is interesting. In the crypt, a series of paintings depict the Visitation and Zechariah in the Temple. The upper chapel is devoted to art relating to our Lady. Some portray events of her lifetime, such as the marriage at Cana, where Jesus changed water into wine at His mother's request. Others portray Mary in later stages of Church history, such as the naval battle of Lepanto (1571), where the intercession of the Blessed Virgin brought victory to the papal fleet and its allies over the Turks — freeing about ten thousand Christian galley slaves and ending permanently the threat of Muslim conquest of Europe and supremacy on the Mediterranean. Another fresco depicts Mary protecting the Church, and yet another shows a scene of the Council of Ephesus (431) which declared our Lady "Theotokos" — the Mother of God.

One very appealing piece of art pays homage to Blessed John Duns Scotus, a thirteenth-century Franciscan and native of Ireland, whose brilliant defense of the Immaculate Conception during a debate at the Sorbonne marks a very important event in ecclesiastical history. Duns Scotus had quite a few other ideas which made him somewhat unpopular among a number of politicians of his time. For example, at a time when kings claimed to rule by "divine right," this Catholic scholar insisted that the state received its authority from the consent of the people.

A visit to Ain Karem should also include a short walk over to St. John's Church, where Catholics of this village attend Mass, as well as a stroll through the wandering streets and alleys of this small community. It is a quiet place which has escaped much of the turmoil of modern life. It is a good place to relax, to think, and to try to sense what life was like in a small Judean village just a few short months before the birth of the Redeemer.

3

Gloria in Excelsis •
East of Bethlehem:
The Shepherds' Field

"AND IN that region there were shepherds out in the field, keeping watch over their flock by night. And an angel of the Lord appeared to them, and the glory of the Lord shone around them, and they were filled with fear. And the angel said to them, 'Be not afraid; for behold, I bring you good news of a great joy which will come to all the people' " (Lk 2:8-10).

It is difficult to think of the Nativity without also recalling the presence of shepherds. Their presence at the Birth of Jesus was vital because they symbolized the message that Christianity was intended for all people — even the poorest shepherd who earned his living by watching sheep through long, cold winter nights.

Thus it is not surprising that many pilgrims make an extra effort to seek out the shepherds' field east of Bethlehem. It is here that common people learned the "news of a great joy." It is here that the angel announced that the joy of Christmas was to be shared by "all the people."

But a pilgrim hiking east of Bethlehem soon learns that there is some disagreement as to the precise location of the shepherds' fields. There are at least four sites that claim this worthy distinction. But this pilgrim believes that the Roman Catholic site is the best candidate — and I'll tell you why.

First, all the Christian churches agree that the shepherds' field was located east of Bethlehem, and this makes a lot of sense. Bethlehem lies just east of a north-south ridgeline that runs the length of the Judean mountains. This ridgeline is the region's watershed, and it has also served as a major highway since remote antiquity. Indeed, it is still known as *Derekh Ha-Avot* — Highway to the Patriarchs — and many biblical communities are located along its route. From the north, there is

Shechem (Nablus), in Samaria, then Shiloh, Bethel, Jerusalem, Bethlehem, Hebron, and then, as the highway descends into the Negev Desert, Beersheba.

Through much of history, it was wise to live close to this highway. This was a path of commerce, and during time of danger, helpers from the king's militia would ride to the rescue along this road. But at the time Jesus was born, the king's militia itself was the prime danger, and prudent people kept a safe distance from these brigands and their main highway. Roman soldiers, including the bodyguards of the puppet King Herod, were notorious for their criminal behavior.

Thus, if the highway lay just west of Bethlehem, a wise shepherd would tend his sheep in the more remote regions east of town. This way, he could better avoid having occasional animals "confiscated" as a special "tax" collected at the whim of whatever corporal developed a taste for lamb stew. Indeed, the Gospels report an incident of St. John the Baptist admonishing such soldiers: "Rob no one by violence or by false accusation, and be content with your wages" (Lk 3:14).

Another important reason for pasturing sheep and goats to the east of Bethlehem is that this land is best suited for livestock. There's a prevailing wind that blows year-round from the west, and in the winter it carries rains and snows from the Mediterranean Sea. The exposed western slopes receive up to thirty inches of precipitation annually, while land lying to the eastern lee side sees only between five and ten inches. Thus, while the west side of the mountains can support thick forests and vegetable gardening, the east side has but a few groves of drought-resistant pine trees and great spaces of open slopes carpeted with sparse growths of wild grasses and shrubs.

There are two agricultural zones on this lee side of the mountains. One is the valley, where the best soil accumulates, and where much of the scant rainfall collects as run-off from the hillsides. Thus the Kidron Valley, which is the main vale east of Bethlehem, is sectioned into fields of grain and groves of olive and apricot trees. Higher up the slopes, where the soil is poor and the rains quickly spill away, there is only scant vegetation — barely enough for sheep and goats to nibble — and a few scattered groves of pine.

While Christians agree that the shepherds tended their sheep to the east of Bethlehem, there is some controversy as to the exact site. The Greek Orthodox, for example, have built a church beside the ruins of a Byzantine basilica in the middle of a broad and level field. Indeed, this is one of the few level places in the region, and for this reason it is not likely to be a shepherd's field. Flat earth is best suited for planting, and at the time of Jesus this field was probably put to the same use as it is today — an olive grove.

The Mormon Church conducts Christmas Eve services on a hilltop on the far side of the Kidron Valley. The site is very beautiful, and kept completely natural with its lovely grove of pine trees. Its single drawback is that it faces due west — right into the teeth of the bitter west wind. Pilgrims at prayer for a few hours on Christmas Eve might relish this exposed position.

The full intensity of nature can be thrilling — in small doses. But we must recall that St. Luke (2:8) tells us that the shepherds "lived in the fields." It's not very likely that they'd have chosen the most exposed site for their winter residence, but perhaps they camped over there during the summer, when the cool breeze is welcomed.

The YMCA tends what is locally known as the "Protestant shepherds' field." While it is doubtful if there were many Protestant shepherds around at the time Jesus was born, the site does have some merit. There is a nice cave which was naturally formed in the limestone bedrock, and the field is located on the higher slopes above the Kidron Valley. But the cave's mouth is oriented toward the north, and thus perpetually sunless. Also, it is located a bit too close to the top of the slope for comfort, especially on blustery winter evenings.

Nevertheless, the YMCA site does have certain facilities which are attractive to tourists. In keeping with the organization's orientation toward physical fitness, they've built basketball and handball courts there, and visitors who acquire a permit from the YMCA headquarters in Jerusalem are allowed to camp overnight in a pleasant pine grove.

The Catholic site is about a half-mile closer to Bethlehem, and if I were a shepherd, this is where I'd tend my sheep. The Catholic field is located above a bend in the Kidron Valley, offering a delightful view. While pilgrims might appreciate such a view for its natural beauty, shepherds would like it because it gives them a better vantage point for keeping track of their sheep and goats. The Catholic site also has a natural cave, but this one is nestled in a lower, more protected position. Its mouth opens eastward — away from the prevailing west wind and toward the warming rays of the morning sun. The cave's mouth also opens into a small, natural glen, where the animals could be gathered during times of danger.

The Franciscans have converted the cave into a very inspiring chapel. It retains its feeling of warmth and security, and its ceiling is of the cave's natural stone — but covered with black soot, evidence of its long use as a refuge by people living in the open hillsides. The altar also has a rustic flavor, and is built of natural, uncut stone. A few archaeological artifacts — an ancient stone jug, the remnant of a column — line the edges of the chapel-grotto.

Outside, the Franciscans have created a charming garden. But contrary to the practice at other sites, this garden does not blend with the landscape. Instead, it is obviously planted by human hands. And this is a constant reminder that the site actually stands upon a naturally barren landscape, a field where shepherds graze their sheep.

A few short steps before the mouth of the cave are the ruins of a Byzantine church and monastery which archaeologists date to the fourth century. The ruins are not as impressive as the basilica at the Greek Orthodox site, but they do have a more pastoral charm lying amid the wild growing grasses and shrubs so loved by goats and sheep.

On the knoll above the cave, a new and very inviting chapel has been built. It's circular in shape, with an altar set right in the middle, and a large dome covering the entire building.

The Holy Land

This dome is studded with hundreds of round glass blocks which catch the sunlight and break it, as a prism does, into cascades of rainbow colors that splash about the chapel. There's an exquisite Nativity mural on the wall opposite the main door, and above, all around the circumference of the dome's base, is written in large, golden letters: "*GLORIA IN ALTISSIMIS DEO, ET IN TERRA PAX HOMINIBVS BONAE VOLVNTATIS — LVCA II 14.*"

The Catholic shepherds' field also has a pleasant path for quiet strolling, and several quiet corners where one may rest and reflect upon the great events that took place here. The gates are open to visitors from 8:00 to 11:30 A.M. and from 2:00 to 5:00 P.M., and there's no opportunity to experience midnight in the shepherds' fields unless special arrangements are made with the Franciscan Custody. There are, however, special occasions when nighttime services are conducted here, and it's best to check with the Christian Information Center in Jerusalem for current details.

These shepherds' fields, incidentally, have a beautiful view of some other fields which should be familiar to Bible readers. This part of the Kidron Valley, lying at the foot of the slope of the Catholic shepherds' field, is locally known as *Sadeh Boaz* — the Field of Boaz. And here, more than a thousand years before the birth of Jesus, occurred one of the most romantic tales in history.

The Book of Ruth in the Old Testament tells the story of a widow named Ruth, a Moabite woman who left her ancestral homeland east of the Jordan River and traveled to the land of Israel with her mother-in-law Naomi. She settled in the hills near Bethlehem, and earned a living by gleaning in the fields of Boaz. She worked hard at her tasks, for gleaners gather only a few grains of wheat and barley left after the reapers have gathered in the crop. These fields are also exposed to the bright sun of late summer, for grain does not grow in the shade. Gleaning is hot, dusty work, and provides just barely enough to eat. But Ruth was content, and faithful to her aging mother-in-law Naomi.

Boaz was moved by Ruth's faithfulness, and the story continues, telling how they came to love each other and were married. The most endearing parts of the story occurred directly below the shepherd's field, on the Kidron Valley floor, which is still largely devoted to groves of olive and apricot, and fields of wheat and barley.

While the story of Ruth and Boaz is idyllic and very gratifying for its own merit, it also has a special importance for Christians, for Ruth and Boaz were among the ancestors of Jesus: "Boaz was the father of Obed, Ruth being his mother, Obed was the father of Jesse; and Jesse was the father of King David" (Mt 1:5-6). The Gospel continues, name by name, through the generations, linking one to the other until the birth of Jesus.

Indeed, this is why Joseph and Mary had to come to Bethlehem under such difficult circumstances. By decree of Caesar Augustus, the entire Roman Empire was to be censused, and to register for the census, every person was required to return to his ancestral hometown. Thus Joseph traveled to Bethlehem — where, generations before, his own family had reaped grain and fruit, tended their livestock, and founded a dynasty which would rule over Israel for centuries.

Pilgrims visiting the shepherds' field would be wise to go with a group or a licensed guide. The fields are three miles east of Bethlehem, not a terribly difficult walk for someone in good shape. But there are several forks on the road, and the sign postings are inadequate. It is quite easy for someone unfamiliar with the region to get lost.

The trip to the shepherds' field is well worth the expense and effort, however. The site itself is refreshing and beautiful. The chapels and gardens are very inspiring. And the mere thought of the events that occurred here, the radiance of the angel and the throng of heavenly hosts singing "Glory to God in the highest heaven, and peace to men who enjoy his favor" — this, indeed, is a vital part of Christmas.

4

Et in Terra Pax •
Bethlehem: Christmas Eve in Manger Square

BETHLEHEM, the "little town of the Judean mountains," the birthplace of Jesus, has become an idealized vision in the minds of many Catholics. Pilgrims planning to visit this ancient community usually assume the town will conform to their expectations. They want the Bethlehem seen on Christmas cards, or the Bethlehem created in Hollywood studios. Somehow, Bethlehem " shouldn't" have traffic problems. It "shouldn't" have rows of tacky souvenir shops crowded around the edge of Manger Square. And the Basilica of the Nativity "should" be a great monument of inspired architecture, and not a dreary, fortresslike edifice decorated with garish ornaments.

It is important for pilgrims to realize that Bethlehem is a lively and developing community tending the many needs of its thirty-four thousand people. Fortunately, it is not a museum piece. *Beth Lehem* (or *Beit Lah'm*) is a Hebrew phrase which means "House of Bread." It has given spiritual nourishment to the world. And it continues to do so.

Although Bethlehem is a town of many shrines, it also has many Catholic schools, clubs, and social-welfare institutions. It is a town visited by thousands and thousands of pilgrims, year after year. They come — some passionately devout, some merely curious — to touch the ancient stones of the Grotto of the Nativity, to see this holy place which is such an important part of their faith, to "be" in the "little town" which has so influenced their lives. But before we queue up behind all the visitors descending into the candle-lit Grotto, let's meet with a Bethlehemite and learn a bit about this community where angels once sang. And let's get a feeling for what Christmas in Bethlehem is like for the common pilgrim.

We visit with Father John Rudy, by no means a native of Bethlehem but by all means a priest who knows much about the goings-on in this town. He's a Franciscan parish priest serving in Bethlehem's St. Catherine's Church, a modern wing of the ancient Basilica of the Nativity. He offers Mass just a few short footsteps from the site where Jesus was born.

Nearness to the holy site, of course, influences him, but foremost he is a Catholic parish priest with some forty-five hundred parishioners to tend. "Bethlehem is a village," he says as we sit together in the cloisters of St. Catherine's. "Aside from the fellowship experience of the church, there really isn't much to do here. There are no movie houses, no entertainment. Public transportation stops at six o'clock." Thus, he notes, the church has become a vital center of community life, with an assortment of women's societies, Catholic Action groups, and other social and charitable associations.

Father John is a native of Cumberland, Rhode Island. He's a New Englander who had served as a parish priest in Winsted, Connecticut, before being assigned to the Holy Land. He knows the Church in the United States very well, and therefore can point out the interesting distinctions for comparison.

"Bethlehem's Catholics are bedrock in the preservation of their faith," he says. "They're a bit more traditional than back home, and Catholics from the West might think this is an old-fashioned parish. But there is a quiet profundity to it. Their faith is very deep."

Bethlehem's Catholics literally pack St. Catherine's Church for five Masses each Sunday. There is very little absenteeism. But St. Catherine's is also a human community, and its people form a cohesive society. The parish provides many important social, recreational, welfare, and legal services which in many other countries are normally provided by the government.

Currently, Bethlehem is located in a disputed territory, and different forces vie with one another for sovereignty. Some call the region Palestine; some call it the West Bank, considering it part of Jordan, while some call it Judea and consider it part of Israel. Today, the territory is governed by Israel through its Civil Administration for Judea and Samaria. Generally, Israel's Civil Administration has a policy which says, in matters not affecting security, local affairs should be left to the capable hands of local institutions — and the Catholic Church is one of these. Thus the Catholic Church, with some government assistance, is encouraged to educate Catholic children in Catholic schools. The Israelis impose several educational requirements concerning the minimum amount of schooling and minimum curricula, but on top of the minimum basic "three Rs" the local church can add all the religious education the youngsters will digest.

St. Catherine's holds all the records most Americans would consider "civil." When a Catholic is born in Bethlehem, the birth is registered at the parish office. And when someone wants to get married, the "license" is granted by the church office. There is no civil marriage in Israel or any of its administered territories. If a Bethlehem Catholic dies without a will, the Church will decide what becomes of his estate. And if there is a will that is contested, a Catholic Church ecclesiastical court will decide who inherits what. St. Catherine's also administers many health and welfare services. Parish groups tend old-age homes, children's hospitals, youth centers, and many other institutions. "The Church here is more a social institution than it is in New England," Father John notes.

The linking of lives on a daily basis has important social implications. The Catholic community embraces its priests as "part of the family" to share birthdays and banquets, illnesses and misfortunes. "Bethlehem's Catholics are warm and hospitable," Father John observes. "It's part of their character. They really want to make priests a part of their families. Their love of the friars is well communicated and well appreciated."

But there is also a community-within-a-community — the Franciscans who have established themselves as a unique and vital order preserving a Catholic presence and identity at sites made holy by the life of Jesus. "There is a mystical experience of being part of a holy shrine," he tells us. In part, he explains, it is rooted in the sacredness of the life of Jesus in this place, but in part it is also associated with the Franciscan heritage. "Franciscans have served in the Holy Land for seven hundred years, and until recently it was a very great sacrifice. They had to give up their own peoples and cultures to come here and serve," he says.

The brown-robed priest recalled that through the centuries, Franciscans were martyred while they protected the holy shrines of Christianity. But these atrocities, he adds, bound the local Catholics to the Franciscans. "There was a great willingness on the part of local Catholics to preserve these shrines, and many died beside the friars. This formed an unbroken continuity of love and blood."

Maintaining active Catholic parishes like St. Catherine's at the various shrines in the Holy Land is vitally important, the New Englander notes. "The presence of Catholic communities helps fulfill the identities of the shrines," he says. "What are Christian holy places without Christian people?"

Failing to see the resident Catholic parish is one of the big tragedies for pilgrims who race through the shrines with tour groups, he says. Christian groups arrive by the busload and rush from one shrine to another "seeing physical places."

"Pilgrims should also settle for a while," Father John believes. "They should take the time to experience the mystical attraction of the shrines and experience the human joy of being close to religious places, the places sanctified by Christ."

The afternoon sun has set behind the walls of St. Catherine's cloisters, and a chill sets in. We get up and stroll through the colonnaded arcade. A statue of St. Jerome, the great scholar and Doctor of the Church, stands solemnly in the center of a small but well-kept garden.

The parish priest recalls that he knew several "lukewarm Catholics" who visited holy shrines and did take the time to sense the holiness. "They stayed on," he says, "and became very devout."

Pilgrims who truly seek the holiness of particular shrines

The Holy Land

typically go through three stages of awareness, Father John tells us. First, the pilgrim is exhilarated by actually being at a place such as Bethlehem, and doesn't take much notice of other people about him. Second, he says, comes a stage in which the pilgrim can become offended by the behavior of other people in the shrine. He becomes upset by irreverent tourists who talk loudly and constantly flash their pocket cameras at every possible subject at the worst possible moment.

But a persistent pilgrim reaches a third stage, even if it means returning to the shrine in spite of the aggravation. This third stage transcends the banalities of public traffic in the shrine and carries the pilgrim to a mystical appreciation of the site. Often, the priest says, pilgrims who have finally experienced the greatness of a shrine start coming in the quiet hours of early morning and early evening, and linger at the site for spiritual enrichment.

"Bethlehem is a great shrine," he says. "But without a thriving human presence, it would be only a museum." The flow of life, both that of visiting pilgrims who have experienced the mystical appreciation of the shrine, and of the town's resident Catholic parish which lives beside the birthplace of Jesus, is vital and requires a constant reflection. "One's faith must develop and grow," he says. "The shrine at prayer is the actual embodiment of faith."

Prayer at a shrine, however, can take many forms of expression. Devotion can be as personal as a quiet thought, or as public as the thunder of drums in a Catholic school's marching band. Both of these, and many other activities, are the prayers of Bethlehem's Christians. And Midnight Mass in Bethlehem on Christmas is perhaps the best known "shrine at prayer" on earth.

Invitations to Midnight Mass are extended only to "special guests," however. Senior officials from the diplomatic staffs of Catholic countries such as France and Italy are invited, along with a big portion of a very large procession which the Latin (Roman Catholic) Patriarch of Jerusalem, Cardinal Giacomo Beltritti, leads into town on Christmas Eve. From one perspective, Midnight Mass in Bethlehem assembles all the "royalty" and "nobility" which happen to be in the region for Christmas. It is a spectacular event of tremendous pomp, reminiscent of the medieval European rituals attended by all the aristocracy of an empire.

But let us be like common pilgrims in Bethlehem for Christmas. All the V.I.P.'s can go into the church for Midnight Mass. We'll explore the venerable old building tomorrow. Today we'll stay outdoors in Manger Square and celebrate with about twelve thousand other festive spirits on this happy, joyous holiday.

Our Christmas Eve starts at noon outside the monastery of Mar Elias on the southern edge of Jerusalem. Cardinal Beltritti arrives in a big, chauffeur-driven Mercedes-Benz limousine. "It must be nearly as long as Noah's Ark!" a friend whispers in my ear. "And probably a bit more comfortable!" I reply. Here, the Latin Patriarch is met by an escort of eight Israeli police mounted on well-tended stallions. Flanking the black limousine, the procession starts its regal march toward Bethlehem. The blue-uniformed police, flashing bright silver buttons and badges, and carrying colorful pennants atop tall poles, are as imposing as any color guard of knights or calvary. Children lining the route wave at the Patriarch and snap stiff but good-natured salutes to the horsemen.

The procession picks up more marchers as it passes Tantur, the Vatican-sponsored Ecumenical Theological Institute standing beside *Derekh Ha-Avot*, the ancient roadway leading from Jerusalem to Bethlehem. East and west of the highway, squads of *mishmar g'vul*, crack Israeli border guards, are scattered through the olive groves and on rooftops to make sure that nobody uses this festive occasion as a target for terror.

Onward they move in stately order, passing cheering onlookers, until they reach the Tomb of Rachel, where the matriarch and wife of Jacob, mother of Joseph and Benjamin, and fortieth-generation direct ancestor of Jesus, lies buried. Here, troops of Boy Scouts and marching bands join the procession before it turns from the highway onto Bethlehem's

Manger Street for its journey toward the center of the town.

More and more people crowd the streets; music fills the air, along with the clatter of horse hooves and the cheering of little children. Another half mile and the procession turns up Star Street, climbing up into Bethlehem's urban district, with its narrow, winding streets and medieval stone buildings. Someone begins to throw flower petals off a roof, and they cascade gently on the Patriarch's auto, on the mounted police, and on the long procession trailing behind. Next, we pass near the Well of David, which according to ancient tradition was held by the Philistines for a while when the young David fought them: "David was then in the stronghold; and the garrison of the Philistines was then at Bethlehem. And David said longingly, 'O that some one would give me water to drink from the well of Bethlehem, which is by the gate!' Then the three mighty men broke through the camp of Philistines, and drew water out of the well of Bethlehem which was by the gate, and took and brought it to David. But he would not drink of it; he poured it out to the LORD, and said, 'Far be it from me, O LORD, that I should do this. Shall I drink the blood of the men who went at the risk of their lives?' Therefore he would not drink it" (2 Sam 23:14-17).

Down through the ancient cobblestone streets of Bethlehem the patriarchal procession advances. Several bands are playing different melodies, and their music reverberates against the stone walls of the buildings that line the narrow street. There is more and more cheering. Cascades of wrapped candies fly into the air and shower down into the crowd. A bagpipe band blares, perhaps with the thought that volume will compensate for practice. There is much happiness.

We link into Pope Paul VI Street and then spill into Manger Square in front of the ancient Basilica of the Nativity. It is 1:30 in the afternoon. The mounted police come to stiff attention as the Patriarch climbs from his limousine. Whole delegations of local clergy and politicians are standing in line to greet His Beatitude. The entire entourage disappears down a red carpet lined with rows of crimson-robed altar boys holding polished brass lamps. Inside, the clergy get ready for Vespers.

Outside in Manger Square, however, processions of bands, social organizations, and youth groups march by in bright uniforms. The festivities have begun!

There's a brief security check for anyone wishing to enter Manger Square, and pilgrims line up along police barricades to take their turns. The process is similar to a standard security check travelers encounter after checking in for El Al (Israeli airline) flights. Pilgrims are separated — men to one side, women to the other — and then shepherded one at a time into small booths where they are confronted by a security officer. They're asked questions, and identification documents are requested. They're also searched for weapons and alcohol. Potential troublemakers are weeded out efficiently. With the security formalities out of the way, pilgrims are free to enter the broad plaza and soak up the festive atmosphere of Manger Square on Christmas Eve with the assurance that there is very little likelihood of anyone marring the joy of the holy day.

Amid all the commotion of tourists and pilgrims and local marching bands, each stepping off in a different direction around the square, are seen hordes of news-media people. Christmas in Bethlehem is an "Event." There are ABC, CBS, NBC, BBC, CBC, and several other letters too, not to mention an entire gaggle of press photographers and a whole bevy of technicians. One group is setting up an enormous television screen, which must be at least thirty feet across, on the northern edge of Manger Square. All of us common folk standing out in the plaza through the afternoon and evening will get to see all the aristocracy inside the church via television. So will everyone else who watches Israel's sole television channel this evening, because the Jewish State now has a long-established policy of live broadcasting of the entire Catholic Midnight Mass each Christmas in Bethlehem. And today, this broadcast is beamed skyward to be picked up by telecommunications satellites, and anyone with a sophisticated "dish" antenna can pick up the signal anywhere in the world.

There's a lot of warm fellowship in Manger Square this

afternoon. Fortunately, it's dry and the sky is clear. On good days such as this, midday temperatures get up to about sixty degrees, while evenings cool down to the forties. Sometimes the weather turns bad, though, and a cold and drenching winter rain can fall. Usually, Bethlehem also has one or two snowfalls each winter, but these are always modest snows and melt away within a day or two. Today, however, the sky is clear, and back in Jerusalem this morning I saw Mrs. Cohen hanging laundry — a sure guarantee of no rain for at least twenty-four hours.

Perfect strangers start new friendships in Manger Square on Christmas Eve. "Pardon me," one elderly gent asks us. "Would you take a picture of the wife and me together?" He produces a small pocket camera and stands with his wife, arms linked, smiling, with the great basilica in the background. "It's simple to operate," he assures us. "Just point and shoot!" With the task completed, he offers a brisk handshake; "The name's Jim O'Neil," he says by way of introduction. We chat a bit, and before parting he insists, "If you're ever in New York, be sure to look us up!" A bit later, we also meet Timothy FitzGerald of Dublin, Ireland, and Emilio Tagliatore of Milan, Italy. A United Nations soldier stationed in Lebanon smiles and says, "Just call me Vanu. I'm from Fiji, in the Pacific." For each of them, and many more, celebrating Christmas in Bethlehem is a once-in-a-lifetime event.

Nightfall comes early this time of year, and as the darkness of evening sets in, an unseen hand throws a master switch and hundreds of electric lights flood their brightness across Manger Square. Little groups, here and there, begin singing Christmas carols. A group of Swiss pilgrims, all holding flickering candles, are gathered near the massive wall of the basilica and begin singing "Silent Night" with the unmistakable accent of "Svitza-Ditch," the Swiss dialect of German. A well-practiced choir of pilgrims from the United States draws a good crowd around them as they begin singing the Latin "Adeste Fideles." On several occasions, outstretched hands beckon us to join informal caroling, and we join in with the singing, fellowship, and making of friends. Indeed, the community spirit of Bethlehem is a bit catchy, and all the thousands in the square seem to be old friends who have known each other for years. They *are*, for their faith has linked one to the other, unseen, across the seas and continents, until we have all joined together in one place on one holy evening.

Around seven o'clock, brightly dressed formal choirs start an evening program on the bleachers erected at the east end of the plaza, right against the walls of the basilica itself. Each in turn sings a repertory of Christmas carols. The local Bethlehem Boys' Choir and a group that has traveled from Nazareth entertain and inspire the pilgrims gathered in the square. Then come the Chorale de Notre Dame from Bordeaux, France, and Trinity University Choir from San Antonio, Texas, and the Rand Afrikaans University Choir of Johannesburg, South Africa, and several others, all raising their voices in the chilling night air to celebrate the birth of the Redeemer and to plead for a bit more peace on earth.

Meanwhile, inside the basilica, there are good gestures toward peace being made. There's a formal banquet hosted by Bethlehem's Christian mayor Elias Freij and catered by a team of Orthodox Jews — the Christmas meal in Bethlehem is strictly kosher. Around the dining table are several high-ranking clergy, several Palestinian Arabs, and a number of high officials of the Israeli government. After the banquet, the Israeli Defense Minister steps outdoors into the arms of a mob of newsmen. Standing near the impromptu news conference, we eavesdrop. "I'm sure you will not be surprised if I tell you that when we talk politics, there are some things we agree on and there are many things we don't agree on," he tells the newsmen. But this Christmas eve, a few disagreements have been resolved by "discussion, goodwill and trying to understand one another. This is the season of goodwill and we should commit ourselves to peace."

What disagreements have been resolved? We are not told. But at least they're talking, and perhaps the spirit of Christmas in Bethlehem is really bringing a measure of goodwill to their discussions. There is more caroling in the square, and small, candlelit processions wander up and down Bethlehem's narrow cobbled streets. There is a spirit of joy everywhere.

By ten o'clock, people holding invitation cards queue up behind the railings leading into the basilica. Those of us without invitations jostle for a good view of the super-large television on the edge of the plaza. We have an excellent view of what's going on inside the church — indeed, a better view than most people who have invitations. An hour later, when all those invited guests have found their places inside St. Catherine's Church, the great organ sounds the opening of the Solemn Office of Readings. The Christmas story begins to unfold. Regal processions, with patriarchs and politicians, ambassadors and clergy, thread into the venerable church. The high vaulted ceilings echo with Latin; incense rises in vapory clouds.

The stroke of midnight is sounded by the great silver bells of Bethlehem, ringing from the stone towers and resounding for miles in all directions. They can be heard far out into the Judean desert, up on the peak of Har (Mount) Gilo to the west, and even in Jerusalem. Now starts the Pontifical Eucharistic Concelebration. It is a formal celebration conducted with smooth precision. Out in the plaza, however, the atmosphere is more informal and relaxed. Thousands of candles are glowing — partly in celebration of the holiday, and partly as hand-warmers for those who have been standing in the chill night for hours. People who were complete strangers a few hours ago are now huddled together, arms linked, faces glowing with happiness.

The Mass broadcast on television dominates the square. The ancient chants and liturgy of the Church echo in the night air. The atmosphere grows more and more devout. It is as if we have reached what Father John called the shrine at prayer becoming the actual embodiment of faith. There is a shared mystical experience, and twelve thousand people do feel it.

One-thirty and the Mass is drawing to a close. Now starts

a solemn procession from St. Catherine's, through a side door, across fifteen yards of stone floor, and down a flight of steps to the tiny Grotto of the Nativity. The Latin Patriarch proclaims the birth of a Messiah. The silver bells ring loudly, intensely. And it is over.

The crowd disperses, but we linger a bit longer, just about two or three hundred yards north of Manger Square, where a view spreads across the darkened desert to the east. The stars are particularly bright here. Bethlehem has a double benefit in being a mountain town on the edge of the desert. The dry air and the high altitude make the stars so much clearer. They twinkle and wish us Merry Christmas.

5

Bonae Voluntatis •
Bethlehem: Basilica
of the Nativity

CHRISTMAS morning Mass with Bethlehem's Arabic-speaking Catholics is an extremely interesting experience which shouldn't be missed by any pilgrim in town for the holiday. From one perspective, these morning Masses are even more inspiring than all the splendor of the famous Midnight Mass (which can be seen on television anyway) because the morning Masses are attended by Bethlehemites. Some of these people are likely distant relatives of Jesus and the Holy Family. Bethlehem, we must always remember, has always been a "family town." Most of Bethlehem's Catholics can enter their parish office and trace their family histories back for many generations — and this is the way it has been for centuries. We need only recall the opening verses of the Gospel according to St. Matthew, in which the ancestry of Jesus is traced backward without interruption for forty-two generations, all the way to Abraham. Bethlehemites know who they are, and who their ancestors were.

The traditional association of people with their "hometown" can also be seen in the Gospel according to St. Luke, who tells us that Joseph was required to go to Bethlehem in order to register in his hometown for the imperial census. Family associations with Bethlehem endure through the ages.

When Joseph and Mary arrived in Bethlehem on that cold winter day nearly two thousand years ago, it's likely that they found shelter with relatives or friends of the family, because there was "no room for them at the inn." So why was there no room at the inn? Simple. Every descendant of David, the shepherd king of Israel, was required to return to the town of David in order to register with the census. The place was probably packed.

The Gospels don't give us precise descriptions of the place where Jesus was born, except to say that it was in Bethlehem and that He was "wrapped in swaddling clothes and lying in a manger" (Lk 2:12). But this only means that the Infant was wrapped in snug, traditional infant's clothes and rested in an animal's feed box.

Our modern perceptions of the Nativity story usually lead us to believe that Jesus was born in a stable. Our Christmas crèche, with its rough-hewn timbers and peaked roof, is as dear to our idealization of Christmas as our romantic image of Bethlehem without parking problems.

It is important to keep in mind that Bethlehem is a mountain town. It is built on the exposed limestone bedrock of the Judean mountains, nearly a kilometer above sea level. It is located on the edge of a desert, and its few trees have always been jealously protected. They certainly wouldn't have been cut down for such an insignificant purpose as the construction of a stable.

The basic building material in Bethlehem is stone. That's what it was three thousand years ago, when David lived here, and that's what it is today. Archaeologists have found that all through antiquity, Bethlehemites tended to build their homes of cut stone blocks set upon the bare bedrock. When an extra room was needed, one frequently used option was simply taking a hammer and chisel and cutting out a grotto beneath the building. These hand-cut cellars served a variety of purposes — a storeroom, a place to shelter goats and sheep when the winter weather outside became too severe, and with a bit of fixing up, a place to offer houseguests.

Would it be unreasonable to assume that upon arriving in Bethlehem and learning that the inn was already filled with others who had also come to register for the census, Joseph led Mary to the home of a friend or relative in his ancestral hometown and asked for shelter? Would it be unreasonable to assume that, upon seeing Mary's condition of very late pregnancy, these people immediately brought the couple into their home and set about arranging the only spare room they had —

their hand-cut cellar? Indeed, this grotto was probably the most appropriate site for the Holy Family. It was cut from bedrock, which meant it was solid and snug, without any of the drafts that probably affected the upper story. It was secluded and quiet, and probably a lot easier on the nerves than the local filled-to-capacity inn. Tidied up, and with a small fire set in one corner, the grotto could have been quite cozy. Fresh straw was likely fluffed, and a blanket spread on top of it, to serve as a couch and bed. An unused manger was found and cleaned as a safe and dry resting place for the expected Infant. The manger would have held the Babe high off the floor, which at this time of year was probably damp and chilly.

All of these probabilities are the impressions which various scholars have developed after visiting the Grotto of the Nativity and studying its layout and construction. Let's visit the Grotto ourselves and ponder what might be seen.

The Grotto of the Nativity is located beneath the enormous and musty Basilica of the Nativity. This great building has an astonishing history itself, but let us be impetuous pilgrims and descend straight into the Grotto. We'll tour the church later.

The Grotto is reached by descending a flight of stone steps worn smooth by the feet of uncounted millions of pilgrims who have visited the shrine through the past sixteen-plus centuries. The Grotto is a rectangular room about thirty-five feet long and ten feet wide. There are two alcoves, one at the head (east end) of the chamber near the stairs, and the other close by and cut into the southern wall. There is a brass star affixed to the stone floor in the alcove at the east end of the Grotto, and it is inscribed with the Latin *HIC DE VIRGINE MARIA JESUS CHRISTUS NATUS EST* ("Here, of the Virgin Mary, Jesus Christ was born"). The star glistens in the glimmer of scores of candles that are constantly flickering in the Grotto, polished smooth every day by the kisses of thousands of pilgrims, and often washed with tears of joy shed by pilgrims who have reached this very holy place.

The other alcove contains the tiny Altar of the Adoration

of the Magi, and according to tradition this is where the manger stood. It is a quiet corner, and the most protected spot in the Grotto.

The natural stone walls of the Grotto are covered with large sheets of asbestos. Centuries ago, these sheets were brightly painted with scenes from the life of Jesus. Today they are blackened by the soot of constantly burning candles, and the paintings are nearly totally obscured. The arched ceiling has dozens of antique oil lamps suspended from it. A careful observer will see that the cables from which the lamps are hung pass through emptied ostrich-egg shells, which prevent mice from climbing directly down the cable and eating all the olive oil that fuels the lamps.

Behind the darkened asbestos, scholars have identified a small chimney bored upward through the rock. Perhaps this provided ventilation for the simple fire that warmed the Holy Family so many years ago.

There's not much else in the Grotto. By our twentieth-century standards, the place is rather primitive — no running water, no kitchen, no toilet, and not even a window. But what seems primitive to us today was quite common in former times.

At the time Jesus was born, no Bethlehem household had an indoor toilet or running water. Kitchens were very simple — an open fire on the floor or, as we have seen in Nazareth, a simple oven cut right into a stone wall. Stone buildings usually had a small window or two, but in midwinter, they were usually sealed shut to keep out the cold and rain. Only the very wealthy could afford the luxury of glass.

It's likely that the water used by the Holy Family for drinking, cooking, washing, and even sterilizing those "swaddling clothes" came from a nearby cistern — a cavity dug into the bedrock, usually about eight feet deep and three feet wide, and often plastered to prevent leakage. Here, winter rains were collected via numerous ducts and channels leading from rooftops and open hillsides. When the rains stopped in late March or early April, these cisterns provided water for the community until the rains began again, in late November or early December.

At this time of year, once the winter rains have started, the cisterns are usually clean and fresh. But in the late summer and fall, after several months of no rainfall at all, the water becomes stagnant, foul, a breeding place for cholera and typhus. At any time of year, however, a wise family boiled all their water before using it. And it is completely plausible that, in the days following the Nativity, either Joseph or someone in the family living above the Grotto made periodic trips to the cistern to collect jugs of water. The water would then be boiled in clay pots over a small fire directly beneath the chimney vent in the ceiling.

We sit for a moment on the step leading into the alcove where the manger stood, and we try to visualize life in this holy place during the days immediately after the Nativity. Tending an infant is a full-time job, and surrounding the great joy of the birth of Jesus, there were also many practical housekeeping chores to be done. Envisioning these chores adds to our impression of Christmas because it gives a sacred event a human perspective. With this human perspective, it is easier for us to identify with the event, and it demonstrates all the more vividly the humanity of Jesus.

There is the door at the west end of the Grotto that didn't exist at the time of the Nativity. It leads to a series of rooms cut from the bedrock in subsequent centuries. Of very great interest is the study of St. Jerome, whose devotion was so intense that he insisted on being as close as possible to the site of the Nativity while he worked. And his labors were monumental. He worked in a bleak crypt about fifty feet from the Grotto. There, with all his books gathered around him, and scrolls of parchment and bottles of ink set before him, St. Jerome produced the Latin Vulgate version of the Bible — gathering into a single text all the various Hebrew, Greek, Aramaic, and Old Latin books of the Bible. Constantly revised, St. Jerome's Vulgate remains the official text of the Bible for the Roman Catholic Church. And this great scholar labored in this dark chamber, so close to the birthplace of his Redeemer, from A.D. 386 until his death thirty-three years later.

There are several other rooms in this labyrinth — an altar to the Holy Innocents, the tombs of SS. Paula, Eustochia, and Eusebius of Cremona. St. Jerome was also interred in these catacombs when he died, but his remains were later transferred to the Church of Santa Maria Maggiore in Rome, where one may also find preserved the manger which tradition claims is the first earthly resting place of Jesus.

Above the Grotto of the Nativity and the complex of newer rooms stands the massive Basilica of the Nativity — the oldest functioning Christian church on the face of the earth. Today, the venerable building is beset by many conflicting claims of ownership and a curious arrangement for sharing it among several Christian denominations.

The basilica was built by order of Emperor Constantine after his mother, St. Helena, made her historic pilgrimage to the Holy Land in A.D. 330. Identifying the site of the Nativity was probably not very difficult for this Christian woman, who also happened to be the mother of the ruling Roman emperor. She was likely very much aware that Bethlehem was a "family town." Indeed, Jesus could trace His ancestry back forty-two generations — perhaps fifteen hundred years — back to the time of the patriarchs, and of Rachel who lies buried on the edge of Bethlehem. Would it be unreasonable that such family traditions were maintained in Bethlehem for another three hundred years, perhaps eight, nine or ten generations? It seems reasonable that Bethlehem was still considered the "town of David" and that many people living there at the time of St. Helena could trace their own ancestry back to the great shepherd king of Israel. And it's also reasonable to suspect that the site of the Nativity was extremely important to the early, secret Christian community in order to preserve evidence of the human life of Jesus. It was here that "the Word became flesh" (Jn 1:14), and the safeguarding of the site of the mystical event would certainly have been one of the foremost priorities for that early Christian community. Preserving the

The Holy Land

physical sites of historic events is one of the most important techniques for preventing later generations from conjecturing that those events were really myths. It is today physically possible to stand in the Grotto where Jesus was born, and all the historical, archaeological, theological, and common-sense arguments agree on this. There is no serious questioning — not among any of the various Christian denominations, not even among the various non-Christian faiths — that Jesus Christ was born in the Grotto of the Nativity in Bethlehem.

Emperor Constantine, being a prudent and soldierly-minded monarch, and realizing that the region is often swept by war and the marauding Bedouin of the desert, ordered that the basilica be built as a fortress. Even the main door was designed defensively — it's but four feet high and requires that nearly all those entering must stoop low and enter one at a time. This makes formal religious processions a bit awkward, but it certainly is an effective technique for discouraging columns of horse-mounted calvary from rushing in. This architecture effectively withstood the onslaughts of centuries. The Persians swept through in the year 614, and fifteen years later the Byzantine Christians booted them out, only to be expelled themselves a mere nine years later by waves of invading Arab armies who carried Islam up from Mecca and Medina. The ancient basilica stood up to continuous waves of invasions, like a breakwater on a stormy shore, for even among the Muslim empires there was continuous strife, and in turn the Damascus Ommayads were deposed by the Baghdad Abbasids and these were driven out by Egyptian caliphs. Yet, Constantine's basilica withstood the turmoil.

The Crusaders captured Bethlehem in July 1099, and during their brief eighty-eight-year tenure, they made much-needed repairs and expansions of the basilica. Like Constantine, the Crusaders saw wisdom in maintaining the fortresslike architecture of the building — and a good thing they did, for in 1187 Saladin, the warlord-sultan of Egypt, led his Saracens to victory over the European knights. Fortunately for the basilica, its "treasure" of religious articles, finely crafted organ pipes, and other valuables was buried when the Muslim victory appeared certain. The "Treasure of Bethlehem," which includes some of the best examples of Crusader-period craftsmanship, lay hidden for centuries until a safe excavation was assured. Today, pilgrims can see these interesting artifacts at the Franciscan Museum near the First Station along Jerusalem's Via Dolorosa.

The centuries following the Crusader defeat saw wavering ties between Christian Europe and the Muslim empires that ruled the Holy Land. In 1482 Catholic King Edward IV of England realized the Mameluke Empire of "slave kings" which was then ruling the Holy Land had degenerated into a constant series of internal feuds and power struggles. Diplomatically playing one side against another, the English king was skillful enough to negotiate a series of vitally important repairs to the basilica in Bethlehem. The most urgent of these repairs was the delivery of several tons of lead to be melted down and used to seal the ancient timbers in the basilica's roof. And because of this the first church of Christendom remained snug and dry for precisely 201 years.

In 1683, the Ottoman Turks were rulers of the Holy Land and they intended to expand their empire. Their main target was Christian Europe. Where the Moors had failed to force Islam on Europe by invading via the Iberian peninsula of Spain, the Ottoman Turks hoped to succeed by throwing their armies hard against Europe's eastern flank. By 1683, they had overrun and subjugated the lands of what we today know as Greece, Albania, Yugoslavia, Bulgaria, Romania, Hungary, and a part of Austria. By then they had surrounded Vienna in a long, bloody, and costly siege.

The vastly outnumbered Austrians, under Field Marshal Ernst Rudiger Graf von Starhemberg, put up a stout defense — but they had one very serious problem. Vienna was running out of food, and even with rationing, the encircled city faced starvation. Nevertheless, von Starhemberg knew it was absolutely essential that he hold out. If Vienna fell, the Ottoman Turks would be in a key position to launch campaigns north against Czechoslovakia, west against the numerous German kingdoms, or — much more invitingly — south into Italy, where they could capture Rome and the Vatican.

The Turks surrounding Vienna had a problem of their own. They were running out of lead, and without lead, they couldn't mold bullets for their attacks. Back went the word through the Ottoman Turkish Empire — scavenge every bit of available lead and send it to the armies at the gates of Vienna! And one Turkish official in the Holy Land recalled that he had a tremendous supply of lead sealing the roof of the great basilica in Bethlehem. Work teams were thrown into action, stripping all the lead from the ancient roof, and preparing to ship it to the front.

Now came the great race and, as some suggest, a greater intervention. On one side, the Austrians and Turks were deadlocked in a bitter struggle, each side desperate for that extra bit of help that would win the day. The Turks needed lead so they could launch a decisive attack, and the Austrians needed reinforcements to break the siege while the Turks were low on ammunition.

The Turks initially had the advantage. Their massive armies were in place, rested, and well-fed. Tons of lead had been removed from the basilica's roof and sent on the way. It was only a matter of a week or two before the lead would be available and the final charge against Vienna launched.

Vienna's mostly Catholic population has come to believe that our Lady interceded. It would have been outrageous if metal which once sheltered the site where Jesus was born was put to use as a weapon of war against a key defense of Christian Europe. That lead, however, was not to reach the Turkish army in time. There were delays along the route, transfers became befuddled in bureaucracy, the "Turkish menace" seemed incapable of efficiently transferring a shipment of war material within the confines of its own territories.

Meanwhile, the Catholics had not been entirely inactive. Catholic King John III of Poland, the famous John Sobieski, quickly gathered an army of twenty-five thousand men and raced them southward across the Carpathian Mountains and into northern Austria. He arrived at the outskirts of Vienna before the Turkish lead came, mounted and personally led an enormous cavalry charge, and sent the Turks into headlong retreat.

Following the rout of the enemy and the rescue of Vienna, the Polish and Austrian kings formed an alliance with the Kingdom of Venice and Pope Innocent XI for a unified push against the Turks. Over the next sixteen years, they gradually squeezed the Turks back — out of Austria, out of Hungary, out of Romania, and out of present-day Yugoslavia. After this, the Ottoman Turks would never again pose a serious threat to Europe.

Meanwhile, the Turks retained control of the Holy Land, and during their declining years of imperial control, they bequeathed a double legacy to the Basilica of the Nativity — a document known as the Status Quo, and a leaky roof. The Status Quo was drafted by Sultan Abdul Mejid, and established precise definitions of rights in the great church for each of the several Christian communities which shared it. For example, according to the Status Quo, at 2:30 P.M. on January 6, Christmas on the Julian calendar, the Coptic Christians are permitted to conduct their Christmas ceremonies in the basilica. During the service, exact formalities must be followed, and these details are written into the Status Quo. One reads: "During this Coptic service in the Grotto [of the Nativity], a Greek Orthodox sacristan and an Armenian sacristan stand on the southern and northern sides of the Altar of the Star respectively. A Latin [Roman Catholic] sacristan also stands on the southern side of the Manger. . . . While this Coptic service is in progress in the Grotto of the Nativity, the Syrian Orthodox are not allowed to stand on the steps of the northern staircase from the floor of the Grotto to the northern transept."

Why, one may ask, are all these Greek Orthodox, Armenians, and Roman Catholics hanging around during a Coptic service? And why must the Syrian Orthodox keep off the steps? Simple. They do this because the Status Quo says so.

And that's why it took so long to fix the roof. The Status Quo doesn't mention who has the right to fix the roof. Therefore, it was presumed that nobody had the right. And therefore, nobody fixed it — for more than three hundred years.

Actually, many people volunteered to fix it. But everytime someone volunteered to do the job, everyone else refused to permit it. This is because there's a great fear that repairing something is related to exercising jurisdiction over it, and nobody holds clear title to the roof.

Over the centuries, the forces of nature worked upon the roofing beams. The Holy Land's long, dry, and hot summers shrunk the ancient timbers. When they swelled again with each winter's rains, they wouldn't match properly. On sunny days, lovely, even inspiring, shafts of light sliced down through the deteriorated roof. Rainy days, however, brought something less stimulating. Christmas worshipers had come to expect puddles all over the church floor — except on particularly cold Christmases. There are even reports of snows sifting through the roof. Even the normally unruffled British became exasperated during their "Mandate Period" (1917-1948) rule in the Holy Land.

L.G.A. Cust, the District Officer during 1929, wrote a confidential report titled "The Status Quo in the Holy Places," in which he informed his superiors in London, "No question more constantly exercised the Moslem rulers of Palestine and took up more of their time than the ever-recurring difficulties and disputes arising out of the circumstances that the Christian Holy Places in Jerusalem and Bethlehem were not in one ownership but were shared and served by several communities." A British survey of the roof in 1935 concluded that repairs were "urgent."

When the Greek Orthodox volunteered to do the job, the Catholics and Armenians protested angrily. Beware of Greeks bearing gifts, they cried. After 1967, when the Israelis began administering the region, they offered to do the job for free and relinquish any and all claims to the Christian basilica. Sounded nice, but nobody believed them. Even if they had absolutely no theological reason for wanting the church, they could always use the roof they repaired as a billboard for El Al Airlines or a matzo factory. Suspicion, skepticism, and mistrust ruled.

Then, when nobody was looking, in November 1983, somebody sneaked up on the roof and fixed it. There are presently two schools of thought in Bethlehem concerning the identity of the furtive roof repairman. Some say the Israelis, unwilling to haggle and dicker with the feuding Christian communities, simply slipped up on the roof and sealed it. Others say that the Almighty, restive after three full centuries of inaction, sent a crew of angels to ensure dry Christmases for the future.

If the Basilica of the Nativity's roof has an extraordinary history, one need descend only to the floor of the Grotto to find an even more astonishing tale. It involves that brass star which marks the precise site of Jesus' birth. It was set in place in 1717 by Roman Catholics. The site, however, is owned by the Greek Orthodox. The Catholics only own the manger site six feet away. Nevertheless, the star stayed in place for one hundred thirty years, mostly because the French could apply some political pressure on the ruling Ottoman Turks.

By 1847, there was intense rivalry between the Roman Catholics and the Greek Orthodox. This was made worse because the French and the Russians were feuding, and the French were backing the Catholics while the Russians backed the Orthodox.

Napoleon III of France was trying to win stronger support at home from the Catholic Church, and to keep them happy, he insisted that the Catholics be given greater privileges in the Holy Land. The Turks, who apparently didn't care which denomination controlled the basilica, bowed to the French demands. They went so far as to take the keys to the basilica away from the Greek Orthodox custodians and hand them over to the Catholics. The Greeks responded by removing the brass star and hiding it.

Russian Tsar Nicholas I was patron of the Orthodox

Christians of the Ottoman Empire — a position gained by the Treaty of Kuchukkainardji in 1774. The Russian tsar insisted that the keys be returned to the Orthodox custodians, but the Turkish sultan, fearing reprisals by the French, refused. Russia responded to the sultan's snub by attacking the Ottoman Turkish Empire.

At first, the Turks reeled under the Russian invasion, losing several important battles, but reinforcements soon arrived. Not only did the French fleet come to join the fray, but they brought along the British fleet, and a few Sardinians, too. Austria declared "ultimatums" — diplomatic demands — against the Russians. And then Prussia started to make gestures of unease against the tsar. Nearly all of Western Europe was mobilizing against Russia. And the fierce struggle that resulted is known in the history books as the Crimean War.

Certainly there were other causes for this war. Western Europe was becoming increasingly concerned over Tsar Nicholas I's expansionist ambitions toward the south. It was obvious he was scheming to absorb the entire Ottoman Empire into his own realm. Nicholas was also well known as a repressive, militaristic, and somewhat blundering monarch. And most diplomats believed the time was ripe to put a stop to Russian ambitions before the tsar's crown was passed along to a more competent strategist. The dispute over the keys to the Basilica of the Nativity, the Tsar Nicholas's imprudent, militaristic response, gave Western Europe the perfect pretext for slamming the Russians back into place.

The Crimean War was marked by gallant foolishness and tragic loss of life, and it revealed much that was wrong with Western Europe's conduct as well as the Russians'. Britain's poet laureate Alfred Lord Tennyson wrote romantic accounts of battlefield bravery and chivalrous valor in poems such as "The Charge of the Light Brigade" — and this served to boost morale at home and encourage enlistments in the army. But others, notably Florence Nightingale, the celebrated "Lady of the Lamp," knew precisely what was going on. She was working on the battlefield of Balaklava, where stupid British officers threw six hundred of their best soldiers right in front of Russian cannons for a very glorious, very irresponsible attack.

Florence Nightingale founded a hospital at Balaklava and organized the first professional nursing care for battlefield wounded despite intense opposition from the British military establishment. The generals insisted that soldiers enduring the pain of their wounds demonstrated the courage and mettle of the British Army, and that soldiers going into battle are braver if they know there are no charitable nurses waiting to tend their wounds. Nightingale responded by suggesting the general staff was a committee of idiots.

Her persistence, with a team of thirty-eight nurses, started reforms which continue to this day. She gathered the wounded from the battlefields, brought them to her two hospitals, treated them, and mended their wounds. Florence Nightingale's own courage started a movement which has not ended the ultimate atrocity — war itself — but it has imposed a series of very basic and necessary reforms. The care of wounded soldiers in properly equipped field hospitals began on the battlefields of the Crimean War. Some decades later, nations of the world further agreed to The Hague Convention, which outlaws "weapons calculated to cause unnecessary suffering" — glass shrapnel, poison gas, mantraps, and other weapons. Then came the Geneva Conventions, which established basic standards of care for prisoners of war, guaranteeing them necessary medical care, essential nutrition, protection against torture, and other vital matters.

The hand of Florence Nightingale can be seen today in the numerous movements to encourage nuclear disarmament, tend the thousands and thousands of refugees trying to escape war, and encourage negotiated settlements to disputes. Before the days of Florence Nightingale, warfare was a noble, chivalrous profession and a legitimate instrument of a country's foreign policy, to be used whenever it appeared profitable. With her reforms, war came to be known as a terrible catastrophe with tremendous misery and suffering. It remains an instrument of foreign policy, but it is no longer as glamorous, or as accept-

The Holy Land

able, as it once was. Florence Nightingale changed the popular image of war, and in doing this enhanced humanity's quest for peace.

And it all can be traced directly to the birthplace of the Prince of Peace, and the brass star which today marks the site.

The Crimean War passed into history. Because of the Western European victory, the Russians backed off and the Turks were required to insist that the Greek Orthodox replace the star. The roof of the basilica is sealed again, and other benefits have crept into the ancient basilica. Yet, peace still eludes the great church, and the various Christian communities sharing the building do so with something less then ecumenical spirit. Mark Twain, the famous American writer, noticed the unease a century ago when he wrote *The Innocents Abroad*, an account of his pilgrimage to the Holy Land. Describing the Basilica of the Nativity, Twain wrote that "envy and uncharitableness were apparent here. The priests and members of the Greek and Latin churches cannot come by the same corridor to kneel at the sacred birthplace of the Redeemer, but are compelled to approach and retire by different avenues, lest they quarrel and fight on this holiest ground on earth."

Ill-will continues to this day, although the Catholics usually try to avoid open conflict. The greatest antagonism today lies between the Greek Orthodox and the Armenians, and it's most obvious during the once-a-year cleaning of the great church.

For one day a year, shortly after Christmas, the doors of the basilica are closed to the public, and clergy of all denominations show up at an appointed hour with brooms, mops, buckets of water, and other cleaning instruments. An Israeli official stands by as referee, with some twenty policemen at the ready to enforce his decisions.

The Status Quo determines which stones may be scrubbed by whom — and the scrubbing of stones, just like the mending of the roof, connotes a certain constructive possession. Thus, during the annual cleaning of the basilica, more attention is usually paid to who is cleaning which stone, rather than how clean the stones actually become.

Cleaning day starts at 8:30 A.M., with a specific number of clergy from each community standing at the ready on their own parts of the floor. The Israeli official asks the spokesman for each community if his people are ready to clean, and only after all say they are prepared does he give the order for cleaning to commence. A year's accumulation of dust is swept into the air with a passion that can only be described as religious. Such clouds are rarely seen outside the central Sahara. But the dust has nowhere to go — especially since all the doors are closed to keep curious pilgrims from witnessing the spectacle. Still, ranks of sweepers pursue their brooms across carefully charted courses with a zeal that could inspire a modern-day Tennyson to pen a new poem about "The Charge of the Bucket Brigade." Woe unto any Armenian who wanders four inches across a Greek stone!

The Israeli referee is quick to impose peace at the first clash of broomsticks — which some monks can use with the skill of professional hockey players — and the official sends errant sweepers back on course.

Meanwhile, over in the northeast corner, stovepipe-hatted Greek Orthodox sweepers hoist twenty-five-foot broomsticks aloft to sweep one section of wall. In this particular area, the Armenians have jurisdiction over the lower part of the wall and the adjacent floor. If the Greeks want to sweep their part of the wall — and thus demonstrate their ownership — they have to stand back in their own territory and use brooms long enough to stretch over the Armenian enclave.

Certain places, like the steps which lead down to the Grotto of the Nativity, are claimed by several communities, and thus are swept by all who have a Status Quo-listed right to sweep them. But the Status Quo also establishes the sequence of sweeping, and who may stand on which stone while sweeping other stones. The Armenians go first, followed by the Roman Catholic Franciscans, followed by the Greek Orthodox. Each of these steps is swept three times in one day, and then left untended for the next 364 days. Fortunately, not many litterbugs visit the Grotto, and usually there are a few pilgrims around who are concerned enough about tidiness to pick up after the rare offender.

Midmorning. The Greeks break out their secret weapon — an ablution of kerosene and sawdust. It doesn't smell like frankincense and myrrh, but it appears to be fairly effective on grubby stones. The Israeli official agrees it can be used, but only in small quantities and at a safe distance from anything flammable.

Off at the west end of the basilica, teams of Greek monks look like commando squads as they swing ladders and ropes up among the rafters. Or perhaps they are like so many angels perched among the roof-support beams and ornate chandeliers. They scrub furiously, all the time climbing closer to heaven. Those working highest in the rafters can justly claim that cleanliness is next to godliness.

In 1984, a minor scuffle broke out between the Greek Orthodox and the Armenians when they disputed who had the right to clean certain stones in a wall located above the Grotto of the Nativity. The fracas was quickly quelled by the Israeli official and his twenty policeman, but the right to clean those particular stones was unresolved.

In 1985, both sides came ready for battle. All started out properly, but as it came time to clean the disputed stones, the Armenians discovered that the Greeks had used the old Trojan Horse trick. They had slipped several muscle-men into the basilica dressed as monks.

The Armenians had been suspicious of the Greeks from the start, and for some time before the cleaning day they were training their own monks in the various arts of self-defense and the deft use of broomsticks. Inevitably, a scuffle broke out over the disputed stones, and twenty Israeli policemen were thrown in to quell the troublemakers. They were not, however, any match for the platoons of black-robed monks, and reinforcements had to be called in.

Meanwhile, the Catholic Franciscans thought the behavior of their embattled colleagues rather unbecoming, and dismissed themselves from the fray. They found refuge behind the heavy doors leading into the St. Catherine's wing of the basilica complex.

Squads of Israeli *mishmar g'vul* came tumbling into the melee, and physically pushed the Greeks and Armenians apart. At the time peace was imposed, some fifty monks were blocked off in their respective corners and first aid was administered to the injured. The most seriously wounded was a Greek Orthodox archimandrite who suffered a nasty cut over his eye. There were also the usual bruises, welts, and contusions common to any riot.

A spokesman for the Armenian Patriarchate later claimed that the Greek Orthodox had intended to encroach on several stones traditionally belonging to the Armenians, and that the Greeks had smuggled in a few toughs to help them complete their seizure this year. When asked by a local newspaper reporter how, in these circumstances, the Greeks suffered the worst wounds, the Armenian replied, "We defended ourselves very well."

The Greeks, perhaps a bit embarrassed at being humbled by the Armenian broomsticks, announced only that there had been a "minor problem" concerning jurisdiction over particular places in the basilica, but that all disputes had subsequently been resolved.

Adeste Fideles •
Around the 'Little Town of Bethlehem'

THE SUN is bright and the atmosphere festive. Christmas pilgrims linger in Bethlehem for a few days and stroll up and down the town's narrow streets to explore its many shrines and Catholic institutions. We gather in the plaza outside the Basilica of the Nativity and begin our expedition by roaming along the southern edge of Manger Square, past all the souvenir shops beckoning for our business. There are racks of scenic postcards, rows of olive-wood carvings of the Holy Family, various saints, camels, and donkeys. Each of the carvings has a sort of primitive appeal, but none of them could be called professional work. They are also selling a number of articles of bright brass, mother-of-pearl, and wood. Crèches, some of them rather ornate, are very popular tourist items, but in all these shops we don't find a single crèche that looks anything like the Grotto of the Nativity. Even the businesses of Bethlehem appear insistent that the myth of the Nativity in a stable be perpetuated. But the shopkeepers are jolly and assure us their wares are made in the full spirit, if not precisely the full detail, of the first Christmas.

Four blocks east, along Milk Grotto Street, we find the Chapel of the Milk Grotto, which is built above a natural cave where, according to tradition, the Holy Family took brief refuge as they prepared to leave for Egypt to escape the murderous King Herod. The Milk Grotto's tradition also says that our Lady, while nursing the Infant Jesus, dropped a bit of milk on the grotto's floor, giving the cave its white, chalky character. Small cakes, which in addition to their normal ingredients also include a few flakes of chalk from the cave, are sold to pilgrims as a therapy for increasing mother's milk.

Strolling back through Bethlehem, we encounter many

Catholic institutions, and we have the benefit of Father George Abu-Khazen as our guide. The Lebanese-born priest leads us over to the Antonian Charitable Society's Home for Aged Women, where we see five dedicated nuns tending about forty elderly women — some of whom have passed their hundredth birthdays. The home is modest and comfortable, and it has a relatively new wing giving it expanded facilities. In Bethlehem, where the term "motherhood" took on a new and glorious meaning, aged women of the local parish are always guaranteed a place to stay and the helping hands of the sisters during their most difficult times.

Our tour takes us by a small housing development where the Antonian Charitable Society has built a cluster of garden apartments for young couples. Father George explains that with decent, modestly priced rentals available in Bethlehem, the town's young people will be more inclined to stay in the community rather than seek bright lights and fortune in the larger cities or abroad.

Up a hill a few blocks away, we visit the Catholic Action Center, where the parish organizes a great number of social functions. There is supervised recreation for youth — sports, movies, and festive parties on holidays. And there are social activities for adults, from the weekly bingo tournaments to the annual parish banquet on the Feast of St. Anthony, when nearly the entire parish gathers for an evening of good cheer and fund-raising. The Feast of St. Anthony is January 17, just a few weeks after Christmas — a perfect time to tap parishioners for generous contributions. By this time, all of Bethlehem's Catholic shopkeepers pretty well know how much profits they made from all the pilgrims during the busy Christmas season. And with this known, they can also estimate how much they can afford to donate to the maintenance of the Home for the Aged, building funds, community centers, and other social and welfare activities of the parish.

Then, there are also the schools — the Salesians' technical school, the Christian Brothers' grade school, and a kindergarten run by the Sisters of the Immaculate Heart of Mary.

There is also the Vatican-sponsored Bethlehem University — the only Catholic institution of higher learning in the Holy Land.

"Thanks to God, we have always had our schools," Father George says, explaining that Catholic schools have preserved the community's identity by providing young people with a Catholic education vital for maintaining the Catholic character of Bethlehem.

"This is very important," the priest says, "because we are very concerned about emigration. It is very important to maintain a Catholic presence in the Holy Land. We cannot permit our shrines to become only places for pilgrims to visit. We cannot let them become museums for visitors. We must maintain our presence here with living, active Catholic communities."

Christian emigration from the Holy Land has been responsible for the decline of many Christian communities for several centuries. A combination of factors, starting back when the Holy Land was part of the Ottoman Turkish Empire, have contributed to the decline. During those Ottoman days, the Holy Land was a backwater province of a decadent empire. Petty officials insisted on bribe money — the infamous "baksheesh" which infuriated Mark Twain during his visit to the region — to perform the simplest task. Corruption existed at every level of government and business. The land was unproductive, and industry didn't exist. Both Christians and Jews, being minorities under Muslim rule, were officially "dhimmis," second-class citizens in the best of times and sufferers of persecution in the worst of times. In circumstances like these, many Catholics who gained the opportunity to emigrate did so.

Early this century, tiny Catholic emigré colonies from the Holy Land existed in many parts of the Western World. They were founded by Catholics who had found success and good life in North and South America, Europe, and Australia. As these colonies began to thrive, they acted as magnets to draw others from the biblical communities of Jerusalem, Nazareth, and Bethlehem. When the Turks lost their Middle Eastern empire in World War I, and the Holy Land came under British mandate, the emigration process continued. Indeed, it intensified.

Many Christians left merely to avoid getting caught up in the violence between Jews and Muslims during the decades of British rule. After the Israeli War of Independence in 1948, Bethlehem was absorbed into Jordan and emigration continued. Jordanian authorities focused nearly all their developmental energies east of the Jordan River, especially in the region of Amman. What they called the "West Bank" stagnated, and Catholic emigration continued.

When Pope Paul VI made his historic pilgrimage to the Holy Land in 1963, he became intensely aware of the emigration problem and the prospect of the Christian holy places becoming empty shrines without the presence of Christian permanent populations to give them a sense of vitality. The Holy See insisted that efforts be made to stop emigration and stimulate renewed vitality of the Christian communities in the Holy Land.

But the real impetus beginning the renaissance of the Christian communities didn't come until after 1967. It didn't begin until after the Six-Day War, when Israeli troops drove the Jordanians out and the "West Bank" was again called by its ancient names of Judea and Samaria. Some Catholics say the renaissance developed in spite of the Israelis; some say it started because of them. Nevertheless, there can be little doubt that Bethlehem today is more attractive and more prosperous than ever before in history. Not until the Israelis took possession of the land were local residents allowed to build institutions of higher education. And since 1967, six colleges and universities have been built — including Bethlehem University.

Our visit to Bethlehem takes us to the Catholic university, where we meet Brother Thomas Scanlan, vice chancellor of the institution and the man with day-to-day authority. The Christian Brother grew up in a tough neighborhood — the South Bronx — and that was excellent preparation for his present assignment. Bethlehem University is often caught in the no-man's-land of the Arab-Israeli conflict, and barbed-wire barricades are as much a part of life here as are faculty meetings. The scent of tear gas is nearly as common as the aroma of brewing coffee. Academia is buffeted by the harsh winds of Levantine politics.

Despite the difficulties, the Catholic university is educating about twelve hundred youths, both Christian and Muslim, and if present trends continue, about eighty percent of them will remain in the Holy Land and assume responsible positions in the community.

"We have helped decrease emigration," Brother Tom tells us, "and I believe we've become an important key for peace in the area, because educated people are more likely to work toward reconciliation and peace." He explains that the university helps its students in two directions — one the traditional academic training, with majors in languages, mathematics, and sciences; the other more practical, producing graduates in nursing, village health work, and hotel management.

Running Bethlehem University also means dealing with the outside world — this school is no isolated ivory tower. And most of the difficulties spring from the Arab-Israeli conflict. A majority of students at this Vatican-sponsored university are Muslim, a fact that is unsettling to quite a few of Bethlehem's Catholics. And within the student population — as at nearly any university on earth — there are a number of political radicals. These radicals, however, distribute Palestine Liberation Organization (PLO) propaganda on campus, an activity forbidden by Israeli law. Occasionally, incidents erupt into heated demonstrations, stone-throwing, tear gas, and the closing of the university for a few days or a week until tempers cool down.

The continued strife has not gone unnoticed by the Vatican. A couple of years ago, Brother Tom had a private audience with Pope John Paul II in Rome, where university problems were discussed. "I knew he was aware of our problems," the brother says, "but I hadn't been aware that his knowledge of the situation was so detailed. He knows very well what's going on here. . . . He wanted me for first-hand observations of the situation, and he made it very clear to me that it is very important to him that the university continue with its work."

Still, occasional disturbances develop. At one time, the PLO flag was hoisted above the roof of the Catholic university, and Israeli authorities moved in, arresting eight student activists who had been passing out literature calling for "resistance, struggle," and the "development of a Palestinian-Soviet friendship." One mentioned "a knife in the throat" of Israel. All were graphically illustrated.

On many university campuses around the world, such literature, flags, and other items are usually ignored. But here, Israeli authorities claim, they are "calculated to incite violence." And in the Middle East, violence is easily incited.

Brother Tom acknowledges the difficulties of administering a university during these violent times, but he's optimistic nevertheless. The university may be rocked by events, but it will survive. "The value of education and academic freedom are integral to the Jewish heritage," he tells us, and in time he expects the Jewish State and the Catholic university to come to more cordial terms.

If the campus is an occasional hotbed, the rest of Bethlehem and the surrounding region are experiencing relative calm and prosperity. The Israelis have generally adopted a philosophy similar to Brother Tom's, realizing that education, health, and prosperity will lead the way to reconciliation and peace. Thus there has been a steady increase in income since 1967, and the gross national product (GNP) of the area has increased at a rate of 8.8 percent per year, in real terms. In 1967, there were twenty-three mother-child health centers in the region; today there are eighty-nine, and they're better equipped. The number of general medical clinics has doubled since 1967, and the percentage of hospital births (as opposed to home births) has more than tripled. Consequently, the infant mortality rate has had a significant decline.

The greatest advancements have been made in agriculture.

Before 1967, Bethlehem and most of the other communities around it had to import a substantial amount of food. Today the balance is reversed, and 177,000 tons of fruit and vegetables are exported from the region annually. Shifting from a net importer to a net exporter of food means better nutrition for the community, and most of this can be attributed to the modern farming techniques introduced by the Israelis. For example, before 1967, the average wheat yield was 176 kilograms per acre, and today it is 660 kilograms per acre. Before 1967, cucumbers were harvested at an average of four tons per acre, but now they are up to ten tons. Citrus fruits are up from 5.6 to 11.6 tons per acre. Barley, which Ruth gleaned from these fields during biblical days, is up from 220 to 712 tons per acre. Indeed, there's a marked increase in productivity in every major crop grown in the region.

The statistics agree. In the past two decades, there have been major improvements in health, education, nutrition, employment, personal wealth, leisure time, and welfare services for the people of Bethlehem and the surrounding region. And because the parishioners of St. Catherine's Church are the single largest segment of Bethlehem's population, they must also be counted among the many recipients of the renaissance.

Debate continues as to why there has been the recent flowering despite all the political tensions and violence. Some say the Vatican's efforts have been paramount. Others point to the Israeli input. Yet others say the people of Bethlehem are doing most of the work themselves. But nobody disputes the claim that the post-1967 period has witnessed the first boom years of prosperity in Bethlehem since the time of the Crusades.

Returning to St. Catherine's, we discuss these issues with Father George. Despite the new affluence and increased cohesiveness in the Roman Catholic parish of Bethlehem, there is still a somber cloud on the horizon. Bethlehem eats well, construction is booming, people are healthy and have the time and money to enjoy leisure activities — but Bethlehem is still a part of the Middle East, and the threat of violence shrouds every day with quiet desperation.

"Peace, that is our first concern in Bethlehem," the parish priest says. "Peace is our first prayer. Since the Franciscans first came here in the year 1219, we have suffered thousands of martyrs. We've bought this land with blood.

"There is a good birth rate here," he continues. "And this helps balance losses. In former times, people simply suffered persecution. There was nothing they could do about it. But today, it's much easier to leave. There are airplanes. And there are relatives abroad who will help. And these things encourage emigration. Although there are many, many improvements, people still want to emigrate," he says.

"Peace is the key," the priest explains. "When there is real peace, emigration will stop. So we must work toward peace as the way of keeping a Christian presence in the Christian holy places. But we have the Cross, and we have the help of God, so even though we are exposed, and even though there is a background of extreme sacrifice, we still have faith."

One of the serious divisions within St. Catherine's parish is which road should be followed toward peace. There are a number of opinions on this issue, but ultimately they are but variations of two basic prospects — Bethlehem must find a permanent political situation as part of either a Jewish or a Muslim state. There simply are not enough Christians in the region to consider pressing for a Christian state.

Many Bethlehem Catholics are willing to speak "off the record" about their views of what the future should be. Violence has consumed too many people who have identified themselves with particular causes — and this includes the Palestinian mayors of Hebron and Ramallah, and the pro-Israeli leaders of the Arab Village Leagues. The following two positions reflect the thinking of two members of St. Catherine's parish in Bethlehem.

"This is the West Bank," reasons one Catholic prepared to be absorbed into a Muslim state. "We are culturally Arabs. Our daily language is Arabic. This is traditionally Arab land. There is only one real Arab alternative for us — we must become part of Jordan. The PLO held some promise for some of us for a while. But now we see that it is very badly divided internally and it is meaningless as a political force. Jordan, however, does have a sound government.

"If we are absorbed by the Israelites," he continues, "they'll kick us out. They want this land. We can say Bethlehem must be Christian because this is where Jesus was born, but they'll say Bethlehem must be Jewish because this is where King David was born.

"Also, you must consider that this is Palestine, and Jordan is also Palestine," he notes. "It is only natural that the two Arabic sections of Palestine be united. Otherwise, we could never exist alone. A separate Palestinian state here on the West Bank would be a failure. We're landlocked and have no access to seaports, but Jordan and Aqaba. We're mountainous, without possibility of an international airfield, but Jordan has much flat land. We don't have an independent infrastructure for education, security, finance, agriculture, health, or any other activity that requires organization, but we could easily integrate into Jordan's existing infrastructure.

"We are Arabs, and most Arabs happen to be Muslim," he says, "so we Christians might as well get used to living in a Muslim state. That's our only real alternative. And if that Muslim state is secular, and Jordan is essentially secular, there shouldn't be much difficulty."

A pro-Israeli Bethlehem Catholic takes another view. "I think we should be permanently and quickly absorbed into Israel," he says. "Christian communities have never thrived in Muslim lands, and there's no reason to suppose we will in the future. The Israelis let us conduct our own affairs, and they don't interfere in any of our internal community business.

"Since 1967, we've made incredible progress," he goes on. "You see the material progress — new buildings, full shops, prosperity, a new university, all in our parish. Our Catholic Action Community Center only began to really grow after the Israelis came. But the progress is much more than what you can see. We now have a better grasp of Western life here, and most of us like it. If we are absorbed into Israel, we will become Israeli citizens, just like all the Catholic Arabs in Nazareth. And that means we'll have the right to vote in meaningful elections. It's as simple as that. Israel is a democracy and Jordan is not. In Jordan, the king decides, and if the king decides to dismiss parliament, which he has done, the parliament goes home meek as mice. If we stay with Israel, the Christian Arab vote could be a significant block, and we could influence the government.

"Remember, votes in the Israeli Knesset are often decided by only three or four seats, and if we held those seats, we'd be in a good position to make great improvements in Bethlehem. Christian Arabs participating in a coalition majority in Israel would do more for the Christian communities of the Holy Land than any imaginable alternative. We could follow the Swiss example, with a canton scheme. Where they have Catholic Swiss French and Protestant Swiss Germans, we could have Arab Israelis and Jewish Israelis. And after all, I won't mind living at peace with the Jews. Jesus was Jewish. His parents were Jewish, very Jewish. St. Joseph traced his ancestry straight back to Abraham, and our Lady's family was very devoted to the Temple.

"The only alternative is a Muslim state," he says. "But what Muslim state? Should this be Palestine run by Arafat and the PLO? Or should it be Jordan run by King Hussein? Remember, that same Hussein was here between 1948 and 1967, and he held back our natural development. He is no friend of the Catholic Church. Prospects of Christian participation in a Muslim state, which certainly would not be democratic, are unclear. The worst I fear is that it would become another Lebanon, with Christians and Muslims at each other's throats. Lebanon has always been like that, and it will always be like that."

Meanwhile, Catholics living in the cradle of their faith face an uncertain future by clinging ever more closely to their church.

Mass attendance is very high. Participation in church-related activities, from parish schools to volunteering with charitable services, to Catholic Action, to the Legion of Mary, to the weekly bingo games, is likewise high. Regardless of the political future of this volatile region, there is little doubt that the Catholics of this parish have the very best spiritual resources for facing it.

Ecce Agnus Dei •
Back to Nazareth, and Cana of Galilee

WE RETURN north, one hundred miles, to the Galilee district and the town of Nazareth, where Jesus spent His boyhood years. We return to the town of the Annunciation to seek what might be learned of the "hidden years" in the life of Jesus. For most of our exploring, we cannot use our Gospels. They are quiet on most of Jesus' boyhood and early manhood. But there are other historical records, plus archaeology, traditions, and the physical geography of the place — indeed, we have several resources that can help us learn more about the Galilee where Jesus grew and matured and started His ministry.

Before entering the town, we climb Jebel En Nabi Sain, which looms above the community's northwest extremity. From here, we have an excellent view of Nazareth, gathered in the semicircular vale at the mountain's base. And further out is the fertile Valley of Jezreel. Jesus must have climbed this mountain many times during His youth. It is so close to His home, so inviting and bucolic — a lovely place for repose and contemplation.

There are several Catholic institutions on this mountaintop today. There's St. Margaret's Girls' Orphanage, and the Convent of the Franciscan Sisters of Mary, and the Salesian School with its extraordinary Basilica of Jesus the Adolescent. The Salesians built this fine building back in 1918, within months of the British victory over the Ottoman Turks in the region. The teaching order used an inspiring medieval architecture with a unique idea of using clusters of narrow columns to support the vaulted roof rather than using traditional massive columns in regular rows. The architecture gives a feeling of lightness which is enhanced by its mountaintop location.

Of great interest is Bogino's masterpiece, a statue of Jesus the Adolescent cut from the finest marble.

The superb view of Nazareth is dominated by the majestic Basilica of the Annunciation. Certainly this wasn't here two thousand years ago, nor were the other Christian shrines, schools, churches, hospitals, and other religious and social-welfare buildings. But while sitting on this mountaintop, and gazing down upon the city, we can imagine at least part of what it was like when Jesus was a lad.

Nazareth of the early first century was a small, impoverished village in the Roman Tetrarchy of the Galilee. Archaeological excavations have revealed that the community was extremely modest and completely Jewish. Herod Antipas, son of the notorious Herod the Great, was the Roman puppet king. But Antipas himself took orders from the Roman procurator, who represented Caesar Augustus in the Holy Land.

Historical records report that the henchmen of both Antipas and the succession of procurators abused their position of power, mercilessly oppressed the people, and constantly demanded unfairly high taxes. Roman military units marched back and forth through the countryside, chasing would-be rebels and seizing any loose wealth in the name of the state. Certainly, St. Joseph in his humble carpentry shop was visited by these armed hoodlums, and like everyone else, he likely let them take whatever they fancied.

Roman oppression sometimes ignited revolt, and many of these outbreaks are documented in several ancient manuscripts. There are even references to them in the New Testament, such as verses in Acts 5 where we read of men named Theudas and Judas the Galilean who gathered supporters and stood against the authorities. In part, these revolts were protests against physical oppression, but they were also revolts against religious oppression. The Jews would not tolerate violation of the Commandments — and particularly the First Commandment, concerning the worship of God.

The Romans seemed to have taken particular pleasure in taunting the Jews with violations of these Commandments.

They made festive spectacles on Saturday, the Jewish Sabbath. They delighted in erecting graven images to pagan gods, and in mocking the Name of the Jewish God.

The historian Josephus Flavius recalls one incident:

"As procurator of Judaea, Tiberius sent [Pontius] Pilate, who during the night, secretly and under cover, conveyed to Jerusalem the images of Caesar known as *signa*. When day dawned this caused great excitement among the Jews; for those who were near were amazed at the sight, which meant that their laws had been trampled on — they do not permit any graven image to be set up in the City — and the angry City mob were joined by a huge influx of people from the country. They rushed off to Pilate in Caesarea, and begged him to remove the *signa* from Jerusalem and to respect their ancient customs. When Pilate refused, they fell prone all round his house and remained motionless for five days and nights.

"The next day Pilate took his seat on the tribunal in the Great Stadium and summoned the mob on the pretext that he was ready to give them an answer. Instead he gave a prearranged signal to the soldiers to surround the Jews in full armor, and the troops formed a ring three deep. The Jews were dumbfounded at the unexpected sight, but Pilate, declaring that he would cut them to pieces unless they accepted the images of Caesar, nodded to the soldiers to bare their swords. At this the Jews, as though by agreement, fell to the ground in a body and bent their necks, shouting that they were ready to be killed rather than transgress the Law. Amazed at the intensity of their religious fervor, Pilate ordered the *signa* to be removed from Jerusalem forthwith."

There were continuous incidents of this sort, and quite often the Romans did not give in. So there was bloodshed.

When Jesus sat on this mountaintop as a growing boy, the entire region was constantly in a state of stress, shifting from one crisis to the next. Perhaps it was here that Jesus saw through the Roman tactics. Perhaps it was here that Jesus prepared for His ministry by developing concepts which simply ignored the Roman chicanery and rendered it meaningless.

The story of the Roman *signa*, for example, sheds a different light on Jesus' famous sermon concerning the payment of tribute to Caesar. Gospel readers will recall that opponents tried to trick Jesus by asking Him, "Is it lawful for us to give tribute to Caesar, or not?" Jesus responded by pointing to a Roman coin and saying, "Then render to Caesar the things that are Caesar's, and to God the things that are God's" (Lk 20:20-25). Modern Gospel readers might simply understand this to mean that Jesus approved of payment of taxes, or, on a more philosophical level, that the state could only demand physical things from its citizens, while their devotion and worship belonged to God alone.

But the Roman coin was a graven image. Indeed, Caesar was worshiped as a god throughout the Roman Empire. Jesus certainly was aware of the incident of the *signa* in Jerusalem. Indeed, His mother's side of the family was closely connected to the Temple in Jerusalem, and His mother's cousin Elizabeth was married to Zecheriah, an important priest at the Temple.

The implications of the Roman coin were much more profound than merely paying taxes. In saying "render to Caesar the things that are Caesar's, and to God the things that are God's," Jesus made a clear distinction between Caesar and God — two separate entities.

Although the Jews refused to accept Caesar as a god, they saw Caesar's image as an idol to a pagan god. Jesus, in effect, told them that since Caesar was not God, the images of Caesar were not idols. Thus, they could be ignored. Paying tribute to Caesar, He said, was not the same thing as worshiping God. There was no violation of the First Commandment in paying taxes with coins engraved with the image of a mortal man.

Sitting on this mountaintop, with its crown of pine and cypress trees, we sense that perhaps Jesus came here during His youth to think of such things. Perhaps He climbed this mountain to get away from the activity of Nazareth and to find peace and solitude, a place to pray.

We descend into the town, which today is populated by about forty thousand people, about half of whom are Christians. Nazareth is, and always has been, a provincial market town. It is a place where peasants from outlying villages bring their crops for sale. It is a place where local artisans manufacture numerous items and sell them in the small shops that line the town's winding streets. Fresh vegetables are still sold here — carrots and tomatoes picked only hours earlier in nearby farms. And it's still possible to purchase locally made goods — even nicely crafted furniture from local carpentry shops. Nazareth, as we know, has carpentry shops which date back to antiquity. But the town is not immune to the twentieth century, and the local shops also carry supplies of Japanese radios, American tape cassettes, and Swiss watches.

Despite the incursion of the modern world, the flavor of Nazareth must be much the same as it was so many centuries ago. And a brief incident at one of the shops gives us a taste of this atmosphere.

We are wandering along a narrow street in the Latin Quarter of Nazareth — Latin meaning Roman Catholic — when we chance to pass a small shop. The shop is but ten or twelve feet wide, and perhaps fifteen feet deep. Its front is entirely open — not a window nor a door, but simply a missing wall. The place is crammed with religious articles, mostly Christian, but a few Jewish and Muslim articles are also in evidence.

We inspect some natural olive-wood rosary beads hanging on a rack. "How much?" we inquire. "For you, only ten dollars!" is the response. "They're natural olive wood!"

"Ten dollars!" we exclaim. "Have they been blessed by the pope? I only want some simple rosary beads for my Irish aunt from the Bronx. I'll give you a buck and a half. Take it or leave it."

"Five American dollars, and that's my final, rock-bottom price," our salesman responds. We don't believe him. Nor are we expected to. "A dollar seventy-five, payable in Israeli shekels," is our counter-offer.

"Israeli shekels!" the merchant exclaims smacking his forehead with the palm of his hand. "Do you know the inflation rate? The money will lose twenty percent value by the time I get it home so my wife can buy groceries for our poor hungry children. Three and a half dollars, payable in American currency."

"Of course I want you to take Israeli currency. This is Israel, isn't it? We are both Israeli citizens, aren't we? You think I have an American Cadillac with a trunk full of gold parked around the corner just because I have an Irish aunt from the Bronx? Two dollars paid in shekels!"

We haggle and negotiate until a young boy of about eight years passes along the street with a brass tray, brass coffee urn, and several glasses. The shopkeeper waves him over. "Be my guest," he says, pointing to a tiny stool pressed against a wall. "How many sugars?"

"*Shukran habibi* (Thank you, friend)," we reply. "Two."

He brings over the coffees — steaming-hot glasses with thick oriental coffee. The glasses have no handles, and my fingertips are frying as I hold the glass. The entire twentieth century has not caught up to this provincial town. We sip coffee and the matter of the rosary beads and price negotiations is temporarily discontinued.

"I am Yosuf," the merchant introduces himself. He's from an old Nazareth family with brothers, sisters, uncles, and aunts scattered all over town. One brother is a politician.

"A communist?" we inquire. "Of course!" Yosuf replies. "This is Nazareth." Indeed, Nazareth is a communist town, with a communist mayor and a communist town council. "Are you a communist too?" we ask. "Of course!" Yosuf replies. "It is very Christian to be communist!"

Yosuf is a balloon-weight communist by Kremlin standards, and his good-natured interpretations of the Gospels and Marxist doctrine wouldn't earn very high marks with the KGB.

A half-hour passes, and the coffee glasses are long since drained. We finally settle on two dollars and fifty cents for the rosary, one dollar payable in U.S. currency and the rest in shekels. I get to pay for the coffee the next time we visit.

And we suspect that this is much the flavor of Nazareth as it was twenty centuries ago. The market is a social center for discussing politics, economics, philosophy, and anything else. People relate to one another on a very human level, exchanging ideas, family concerns, and good will as well as the buying and selling.

Did Jesus walk through these streets, sent on errands by His mother, and haggle with similar merchants. We suspect that He did. And we also suspect that in those days, pious Jewish shopkeepers might have preferred local coins rather than Roman coins with the emperor's image.

We wander eastward a bit, threading through more narrow streets, paved with blocks of limestone. Most of the buildings are two and three stories high, also built of limestone, with the street floors devoted to shops and businesses. We emerge on Pope Paul VI Road, the main street of town, and turn left until we come to a massive stone fountain gurgling with water. This is Mary's Well, and it has served the families of this Galilean town for thousands of years. Tradition says that Mary visited this well almost daily during the decades that the Holy Family lived here. And to this day, the women of Nazareth still come to the fountain to collect water in clay jars which they balance gracefully on their heads.

The fountain is fed by a small aqueduct which flows from the nearby St. Gabriel's Church, which is built over a spring. It's a Greek Orthodox church, and according to this denomination, it is the true site of the Annunciation. Roman Catholics differ on this point, and with good reason.

A ten-minute walk southward takes us near the Basilica of the Annunciation to St. Joseph's Church. The shrine marks the traditional site of Joseph's carpentry shop. Archaeological excavations have demonstrated that the church stands on the site of an older Crusader church, and this, in turn, was built upon Byzantine ruins. Ancient cisterns have been discovered in the bedrock, along with a small pool paved with mosaics.

Also, several underground silos were found, and evidence indicates that during ancient times these were used to store olive oil and grain.

Did St. Joseph pursue his trade here? Yes, we believe so. The site has been venerated for centuries. And certainly Jesus helped his father here, stacking boards, sharpening tools, and generally helping with the chores one might expect of a good son of a good carpenter.

Five minutes from here is another shrine — *Mensa Christi* — the Table of Christ. Here, the Franciscans have built a small chapel around a block of limestone which they say served as the table used by Jesus and the apostles when He appeared to them after the Resurrection.

There are scores of other shrines and Christian institutions scattered around Nazareth, and strolling leisurely, we pass many of them. There are the Frères School and Casa Nova, and the lovely Carmelite Convent. There are the Little Sisters of Jesus, the Convent of St. Claire, the Franciscan Monastery, and so many other structures. One seems a bit out of place. Our eye catches a sign — "FRANK SINATRA BROTHERHOOD CENTER," and upon our asking within, it appears that the famous American singer contributed handsomely to the building fund of this social center to encourage brotherhood and sportsmanship among Nazareth's youths.

One of Nazareth's most important shrines is often missed by pilgrims. This is the Synagogue Church, a simple little building located back in the market district amid bustling crowds of merchants and shoppers. It belongs to the Greek Catholic Church, which has built a new church beside the ancient ruin.

There is general agreement among scholars and archaeologists that this building served as Nazareth's synagogue when Jesus lived here. They agree that Jesus studied the Torah and the Psalms and the Prophets here, and this is where He attended Saturday worship services.

Scholars also agree that this is the synagogue referred to in the Gospels: "And he came to Nazareth, where he had been brought up; and he went into the synagogue, as his custom was, on the sabbath day. And he stood up to read, and there was given to him the book of the Prophet Isaiah. He opened the book and found the place where it was written: 'The spirit of the Lord is upon me, because he has anointed me to preach good news to the poor. He has sent me to proclaim release to the captives and recovering of sight to the blind, to set at liberty those who are oppressed, to proclaim the acceptable year of the Lord.' And he closed the book, and gave it back to the attendant, and sat down. And the eyes of all in the synagogue were fixed on him. And he began to say to them, 'Today this scripture has been fulfilled in your hearing.' And all spoke well of him, and wondered at the gracious words which proceeded out of his mouth and they said, 'Is not this Joseph's son?' " (Lk 4:16-28).

Jesus went on to proclaim in this synagogue that "no prophet is acceptable in his own country." And He illustrated this by citing examples such as Elijah taking refuge in Phoenicia, outside of Israel, and Elisha curing a Syrian leper although there were many lepers also in Israel. These examples must have touched the people in the synagogue in a sensitive place, for He seemed to be preaching the unworthiness of Israel: "And they rose up and put him out of the city, and led him to the brow of the hill on which their city was built, that they might throw him down headlong. But passing through the midst of them he went away" (Lk 4:29-30).

Visitors at the south end of Nazareth may notice the Convent of *Notre Dame de l'Effroi* — "Our Lady of Fear" — where the French *Soeurs Clarisses* keep vigil on the traditional site where Mary shook with fear when she saw the angry crowd chasing her Son out of town, intent on throwing Him over a cliff. Continuing south, the main road passes by a forested hillside with a steep cliff, known for centuries as *Mons Saltus Domini* — "the Leap of the Lord Hill."

Jesus was prophetic when He said that prophets aren't accepted in their own land. In the coming centuries, while much of the Galilee gradually converted to Christianity, Nazareth remained staunchly Jewish, and it was only after the Arab invasions, when all the Jews were either massacred or sold into slavery, followed by centuries of desolation, that the Crusaders restored the community and installed a Christian population.

The first Christian buildings in Nazareth were built by order of Emperor Constantine in A.D. 326. But the Christians were there only because they had the government on their side. Otherwise, the great majority of the population was Jewish. Two and a half centuries later, it was still Jewish, and a Christian pilgrim of the year 570 observed that "the charm of the Hebrew women of this city [Nazareth] is greater than those of the entire land."

Both Christian and Jewish communities of Nazareth were destroyed by the Arab invasion of 636, and the entire town was reduced to rubble. Nobody was permitted to rebuild Nazareth until more than four hundred years later, when the Crusaders conquered the land and restored Christian holy places. The restoration was short-lived, however, and less than a century after the Crusader conquest, the European knights fell before the sword of Islam at the Horns of Hittin, a battlefield about fifteen miles northeast of Nazareth. After this defeat, the Christian community of Nazareth was massacred and all Christian buildings demolished.

Only in the sixteenth century were Franciscan monks permitted to return to Nazareth, to live within its rubble, and begin the slow restoration of Christian presence in a community made holy forever by the life of Christ.

There's a road leading northeast from Nazareth, and anybody visiting the boyhood home of Jesus should make a short side-trip down this pleasant highway, for, some four miles across the Galilean hills, we come to the village of Cana, where Jesus performed His first miracle.

John's Gospel relates how Jesus and Mary were attending a wedding feast in this village when the hosts ran out of wine, and Mary solicited her Son's help. Although Jesus thought it premature to begin His ministry — "My hour has not yet come," He said (Jn 2:4) — He relented for his mother's sake.

Jesus performed His first miracle by changing water into wine, thus consecrating what many believe to be the first Christian wedding.

Father Pierre, a French-speaking Franciscan, is tending the Catholic shrine at Cana on the day we visit. He's an elderly fellow, with a sprightly smile and an air of enthusiasm. He unlocks the front doors and leads us into a shrine which is divided into two levels. The upper level is organized as a Catholic chapel with a traditional altar. The lower level, however, is a crypt with an interesting treasure of artifacts from the time of Jesus. Father Pierre claims that there is an excellent likelihood that these same artifacts could have been in this very room when Jesus performed His first miracle here.

It would have been much easier to corroborate this tradition if St. John's Gospel had given us the name of the owner of the house where the wedding feast was conducted, for this could have been matched against an ancient Aramaic inscription set in the remains of the mosaic floor of the crypt dating from the Roman period: "Honored be the memory of Yoseh, son of Tankum, son of Buta, and his sons, who made this mosaic; may it be a blessing for them. Amen."

A most interesting artifact is a large stone water jar found at the site. It dates from the time of Jesus, although the idea behind the stone water jug is actually much older — and it's an idea which is still commonly used in the Holy Land today. The jug is carved from porous stone, and therefore tends to "sweat" when it's filled with water. The moisture collecting on the outside of the jug evaporates in the dry air and, since evaporation is a cooling process, the large volume of water in the jug remains quite cool, even on the hottest summer day.

The religious significance of this stone jug, however, is noted in the Gospel of St. John, where we read the miracle at Cana was performed by using water collected in "six stone jars." Each jar, or jug, would contain about twenty gallons, thus indicating a volume like that which St. John described.

Roman columns, capitals, friezes, and mosaics all contribute to the evidence that the shrine was built upon the house of a wealthy family of the first century A.D. — precisely the sort of people who could have thrown a very large party for their daughter's wedding. And we know this was a large party because of the very large store of wine used. The Gospels tell us that the hosts ran out of wine during the wedding feast and Jesus converted at least one hundred twenty gallons of water into wine to make up for the shortfall. That's a tremendous amount of wine and suggests a very large party indeed!

The present church in Cana dates from only 1879, although the Franciscans have tended previous shrines on this spot since 1641. The Franciscan traditions linking the site with the miracle can be traced back through Friar Niccolo of Poggibonsi (1345), documents from the time of Charlemagne (808), and St. Willibald (726). But it was only recently, in 1965, that archaeological excavations into the shrine's foundations revealed the treasures of the building's predecessors, or, as Father Pierre notes, "It's just another case of the archaeologists confirming what Catholics have believed all along."

The Franciscans have a few other things to say about the shrine. The most important is printed in a single paragraph of a notice posted at the shrine. It states that they believe the shrine to be built on the precise location of Jesus' first miracle, and "Jesus performing that sign made manifest His divine power and glory, and, at the same time, consecrated the conjugal union, foundation of the family, which is already a small church in itself. The Virgin Mary, with her affective intervention in her Son's miracle, reveals herself as our Mediatrix and most provident Mother, who obtains for us her children the graces and help necessary for our spiritual and secular life."

Today, about eight thousand people live in this ancient village of Cana, but only twenty-five hundred of them are Christian. The rest are Muslim villagers. Through most of the year, Cana is little more than a rest stop on the main road from Nazareth to Tiberius on the Sea of Galilee. But on the Second Sunday in January, when chill winter winds whip over these Galilean hills, tens of thousands of pilgrims come to celebrate the feast of Jesus' first miracle. Many of these pilgrims travel all the way from Europe and America, but most are Catholics native to the Holy Land, coming from Jerusalem, Bethlehem, and nearby Nazareth. And a few have only a few minutes' walk through Cana's narrow cobblestone streets from their homes in this biblical town to the shrine which, on this feast day, becomes the center of attention for Catholics around the world while they listen to the words of the Holy Gospel.

Domine . . . Perimus! •
Around the Sea
of Galilee

EASTWARD FROM Nazareth and Cana, we roll across the open hills of the Galilee. Many are planted with field crops, although most are simply open meadow used for grazing flocks of goats and sheep. We pass by several Arab villages and Jewish kibbutzim. To our left, we see the barren saddle-shaped Horns of Hittin. Between these twin peaks, the Crusader armies of the Holy Land were crushed by Saladin and his Muslim legions in 1187. The Crusader kingdom rapidly declined after this battle, never to regain its former glory.

Eastward yet we drive until we reach the crest of a steep hill. Here, at about 650 feet above sea level, we look out at the magnificent landscape. Right before us is the Sea of Galilee, lying at 700 feet below sea level — that is, about 1,350 feet below our feet. It is more of a large lake than a sea: it measures only eight miles across and thirteen miles long. Its sixty-four-square-mile surface is less than one percent of the area of Lake Ontario — the smallest of the Great Lakes.

The Sea of Galilee's ancient Hebrew name is Lake Kinneret, derived from "*kinnor*," the harp which David played as a shepherd boy. In the beachfront cafés at Tiberias, the biggest community on the lake, there is a popular debate over whether the name comes from this lake's harplike shape, or whether it comes from the gentle music of the evening breeze and tiny waves which wash upon its rocky shore.

From our vantage above the Sea of Galilee we can see its entire area and many of the communities we'll be visiting in the coming pages: Magdala, the home of Mary Magdalene; Ginnosar or Gennesaret, the plain where Jesus preached; Et-Tabgha, famous for its "five loaves and two fishes"; Capernaum or Capharnaum, the home of many apostles, where Jesus began His public ministry; the Mount of the Beatitudes, site of the beautiful Sermon on the Mount; Bethsaida, where Jesus healed the blind man; and Kursi, where Jesus cast demons from a tormented man.

Rising above the opposite shore are the solemn Golan Heights, a land of tragic history. To our right, the Sea of Galilee spills out into the Jordan River, which wanders southward another sixty miles or so to the Dead Sea. Along that route are sites associated with the baptism of Jesus, the wandering in the desert, and other important episodes of the Gospels. Some archaeologists have even claimed to have found the remains of the Garden of Eden there — but more about this in a later chapter. For now, let us drive down this great hill to the town of Tiberias, built in A.D. 18 by Herod Antipas and named in honor of the Roman Emperor Tiberius.

Today, Tiberias is a popular resort town with many tourist attractions. Its tropical climate makes it a year-long haven for vacationers, and its carefree ambiance makes it particularly popular with informal visitors. Tiberias is also a small but ancient city, rich in history, with many ruins dating back to the Roman, Byzantine, Arab, and Crusader periods.

Hammat Tiberias is a series of hot springs which were fed into Roman baths back at the time of Jesus in Galilee. The ruins can still be seen, including their lovely mosaics. Not far away, newer baths have been built, and people from around the world come to rest in their waters. Their mineral concentrations and temperatures are said to be excellent treatment for rheumatic ailments and nervous disorders.

St. Peter's Church is built right at the water's edge. This Franciscan house of worship has a most interesting history, which starts back in the Crusades. But after the Muslim conquests, the building was converted into a mosque, and then went into decline to be used as a *khan* or caravansary, a place where camels and freight and donkeys and herdsmen took shelter at night or in times of trouble. Later, the Catholic Church reacquired the building, restoring it for use as a church, and in the past century, it has undergone three major renovations. Of particular interest is the nave, which points east, toward the Sea of Galilee, and is designed in the shape of a fishing boat's bow. Outside in the courtyard is a monument erected by Free Polish soldiers, who were stationed here during World War II to help defend the Holy Land against threats from the Axis powers.

Wandering around Tiberias, we also come across remnants of the city's old walls — massive blocks of black basalt stone — but these are in a state of general disrepair. At the northwest corner of the walls is the old "Northern Citadel" of the Crusaders, today a picturesque, restored complex with a number of artists' studios, gift shops, and restaurants. The outside walls are overgrown with vines and flowers.

There are two mosques worth visiting in Tiberias. Jami el-Bahr, near the water's edge, is an old structure built on Crusader foundations which today serves as the community's archaeological museum. Not far away is the Great Mosque, built more than two centuries ago by Sheikh Dahr el-Omar and still in daily use as a hou1se of worship. Its domed arcades and towering minaret are fine examples of classical Islamic architecture.

Tiberias also has a rich Jewish h1eritage, and much of this can be read on the tombs of the famous sages who are buried her1e. After the Romans destroyed J1erusalem, Tiberias became the center of Judaic scholarship and teaching. The names of the great sages buried here are familiar to many Christian scholars who have studied their wisdom: Rabbi Moses ben Maimon, known also as Maimonides or the Rambam, was one of the greatest intellectuals of history, as was Rabbi Me'ir Ba'al Hanes, "the Illuminator." The eminent Yohanan Ben Zakkai, Rabbi Eliezer the Great, and Rabbis Ammi and Assi are all buried here in what must be the Jewish equivalent of Egypt's fabled Valley of the Kings. Here, however, the Jews have not established a special sanctuary to revere the memory of their political leaders, but instead have consecrated the earth to honor their greatest religious leaders through the centuries.

Of special appeal is the white tomb of Rabbi Akiva, located on the hillside above town. Akiva was born to a poor farm family near Jerusalem about two decades after the Resurrection. As a boy, he tended the flocks of a wealthy family in the region and, as such stories go, fell in love with that family's daughter, Rachel. But Rachel would not wed an ignorant and illiterate shepherd boy. Therefore Akiva learned to read. They eventually married, and Akiva went on to become one of the most esteemed Jewish scholars of all time, blending a great deal of intellectual clarity and heartfelt love into his teachings. He was a highly respected sage throughout the land when, in A.D. 135, the Jews revolted for a third time against Roman rule. Akiva preached against Roman paganism and force of arms, and for this, at approximately age eighty-five, he was martyred by the soldiers of Emperor Hadrian.

After all this hiking around Tiberias through Catholic churches, Muslim mosques, and Jewish cemeteries, one develops an appetite, and there's but one thing to do — find an appropriate restaurant.

Such a restaurant is easy to find. It's located down near the seashore with a lovely view of Fisherman's Anchorage. And indeed, fishermen do still anchor their boats here. A pilgrim in the Holy Land might be presented with a large menu, but there's only one dish which can be considered. "St. Peter's fish," we tell the waitress.

This particular species is known to scientists as *Tilapia galilea*, and today it is — just as it was two thousand years ago — the most common fish swimming in the Sea of Galilee. This is the type of fish that filled the nets of the apostles.

One fishing expedition, recorded by St. Luke, was particularly memorable: ". . . When he [Jesus] had ceased speaking, he said to Simon, 'Put out into the deep and let down your nets for a catch.' And Simon answered, 'Master, we toiled all night and took nothing. But at your word I will let down the nets.' And when they had done this, they enclosed a great shoal of fish; and as their nets were breaking, they beckoned to their partners in the other boat to come and help them. And they came and filled both the boats, so that they began to sink" (Lk 5:4-7).

That is one fish story in which the ones that got away were very few indeed. After this event, the apostles gave up fishing to become "fishers of men."

In St. Luke's Gospel, the apostles were probably using the floating-seine-net fishing system, one of the three types of fishing mentioned in the Gospels. With the floating seine, a net is set out in the water hanging from a series of floats. Gradually, the ends of the net are brought together, forming a large pocket. This is gradually drawn together, forcing the fish trapped inside into a smaller and smaller space until the entire contents of the net can be lifted into a boat.

The other types of fishing mentioned in the Gospels include the common hook and line (see Mt 17:27) and weighted casting nets (see Mt 4:18). The weighted casting nets are used in shallow water. They can be tossed into the air and, because of the weights along their edges, sink quickly to the bottom, trapping fish between the net and the bottom of the lake.

The St. Peter's fish is extremely interesting to ichthyologists. It is an oviparous, or egg-laying, fish of the cichlid group. Unlike other fish, this species takes special care of its eggs and young. Once the eggs are laid, the parents remain in the immediate vicinity as they mature. If danger approaches, the parent fish scoop the eggs up in their mouths and swim away to safety. And later, once the danger has passed, the eggs are deposited back in their original place.

Similar protection is offered to the small fry once the eggs hatch, and if danger threatens, the tiny hatchlings swim right into the safety of the parents' mouths until the area is again safe.

This system of protecting eggs and young from predators must be very useful, because the St. Peter's fish is certainly the most numerous fish in the Sea of Galilee.

There are other fish, for sure — two dozen species have been identified — and thoughtful scientists have given them amusing names. *Haplochronis josepii flavii* is a small fish named for Josephus Flavius, a Jewish historian who lived in this region shortly after the time of Jesus, and indeed, some of Josephus' works describe other fish of this sea. *Tristramella simonis* carries a double honor. Its first, or "genus," name honors Canon H.B. Tristram, an Anglican clergyman who explored the natural history of the Bible back in the nineteenth century. The *simonis* part of the name is for Simon, called Peter.

If you come along the shores of the Sea of Galilee at nighttime, there's a good likelihood that you'll see small lights twinkling out on the water, bobbing up and down with the gentle waves. These are fishing boats, and they're using the same techniques that were popular two thousand years ago when the apostles were still fishers of fish. Recall the Gospel mentioned earlier, when St. Peter complained "we toiled all night and took nothing." The apostles were surely sitting in the boats all night long, riding quietly and burning lights along the sides of their boats. A net was set out in the water and the fishermen waited for the light to attract the fish to the surface — just as a light may attract mosquitos and moths. When several fish are seen near the surface, the nets are pulled snug, trapping them in the seine.

The Gospels are filled with stories of fish. There is the loaves-and-fishes miracle, of course (see Jn 6:5-13; Mt, Mk, Lk passim), and we may recall that Jesus instructed St. Peter to find tax money in the mouth of a fish (see Mt 17:27). The metaphor becomes stronger in passages such as: "Again, the kingdom of heaven is like a net which was thrown into the sea and gathered fish of every kind; when it was full, men drew it ashore and sat down and sorted the good into vessels but threw away the bad" (Mt 13:47-49).

So much reference to fish was very useful to Jesus because His first apostles, as well as the first communities that heard Him, were all fishermen. They understood very well all the symbols and metaphors of fishing, and by using examples from their daily lives, Jesus was able to explain to them the "good news" of His ministry.

Fish became so associated with the early Christian community that a stylized fish became nearly as common as a cross in the symbolism of the early Church. Early Christians, fearing persecution by the Romans, had to be very discreet, and so they developed a series of codes to identify themselves. One of these codes was a simple, stylized fish, like this: ⌒◁ .

They also used the Greek word for fish: ΙΧβΥΣ,

This was understood as an acronym for the Greek phrase that means "Jesus Christ, Son of God, Savior":

$$Ιησος \ Χιρστος \ βεου \ Υιος \ Σωτηρ$$

The waitress finally brings out St. Peter's fish with a nice side order of oriental salads — *homus, tahina,* turkish salad — and a platter of fresh, warm pita bread. This fish is so symbolic, how can we dare eat it? But we do anyway, with great relish, and it isn't even Friday. After all, we theorize, any fish that was good enough for Jesus to feed the multitude is certainly good enough for us.

Well-fed and relaxed, we continue our journey by driving north along the edge of the Sea of Galilee. It is a pleasantly mild spring day; the countryside is lovely, and the sea calm. There are picnickers making their lunches beneath the eucalyptus trees along the beach, and our eyes are caught by a most extraordinary sign: "DANGER — Beware of Western Sweeping Winps." "Winps?" Curious. We drive another mile or so, and there it is again "DANGER — Beware of Western Sweeping Winps." But what's a "Winp"? And why are they sweeping? And why from the west?

Our investigation reveals that a Winp is a simple typographical error made by a government employee who repeated it three dozen times on as many signs along this shore of the Sea of Galilee. He should have printed "Winds," and people recalling the miracle of the calming of the storm already know something about these notorious gales: "And when he [Jesus] got into the boat, his disciples followed him. And behold, there arose a great storm on the sea, so that the boat was being swamped by the waves; but he was asleep. And they went and woke him, saying, 'Save [us], Lord; we are perishing!' And he said to them, 'Why are you afraid, O men of little faith?' Then he rose and rebuked the winds and the sea; and there was a great calm'' (Mt 8:23-26).

Those sudden storms still surprise people along the Sea of Galilee, and every year a few fishing boats are lost. In fact, two years ago a small seaplane landed on this lake, and without warning, another gale came howling from the west, sweeping across the face of the water, and spilling the aircraft over. Fortunately, nobody was injured, but the airplane was a loss. Vacationers are advised —'at the first sign of a strong westerly wind, get clear of the water.

About four miles north of Tiberias, a gravel road turns off to the west and brings us up to the ruins of Migdal. *Migdal* is a Hebrew word that means "tower" — but when you're standing in the middle of this ancient Galilean village, the name somehow seems inappropriate. If anything, it's the surrounding landscape that towers. The village itself was built on the lower slopes of Mount Ravid.

Migdal is a very 1modest tower. Indeed, it is about six hundred feet below sea level — not very towering at all. Unlikely as it may seem, however, this is an excellent place for towers — both real and figurative. The real tower was built here about thirty-two centuries ago. After Moses led the Children of Israel back into the Promised Land and Joshua had secured it, this area was assigned t1o the Tribe of Naphtali, and here was built Migdal-El, the Tower of God (Josh 19:38). Although the present Migdal is situated about a half-mile from the shoreline of the Sea of Galilee, ancient Migdal-El was a fishing village close to the water's edge. Archaeologists hypothesize that the original Tower of God also had a practical use — it was probably a lighthouse that guided fishermen back to their village at the end of their night fishing.

Another similar tower likely existed here at the time of Jesus' ministry, when the village was known as Magdala. Gospel readers may recall that after Jesus performed the miracle of the loaves and the fishes, ''sending away the multitude, he got into the boat and went to the region of Magadan [Magdala]''

The Holy Land

(Mt 15:39). Certainly there were docking facilities here, and probably a light tower, and judging from the description of one of its inhabitants, the place might have had a rowdy reputation.

People living in Magdala were called Magdalene, and most scholars agree that this was the hometown of "Mary, called Magdalene, from whom seven demons had gone out" (Lk 8:2). Mary, once she reformed, was among the most devoted of Jesus' followers. And in the figurative interpretation of her hometown, we find that she became something of a tower as foremost among the women who ministered to Jesus. Mary Magdalene was a tower of courage and devotion. She was an unlikely tower — as unlikely as a town six hundred feet below sea level being called "tower." But this unlikeliness actually increases the greatness of both.

Mary Magdalene was a most interesting character, a person driven to extremes, whether in sin or piety. Many people speculate on just who Mary Magdalene was, and theologian J.R.P. Sclater offers a most interesting theory. He notes that Mary is often portrayed as a beautiful young girl led astray by lustful and evil men. But that classical image was reversed by an Italian sculptor who depicted her as a wretched old hag, malicious and ugly. This image, Sclater contends, may be more appropriate because it demonstrates that the love of Jesus went beyond those who were merely poor, miserable, and lost — the victims of circumstances. The love of Jesus reached further, to the depraved, the cruel, and the corrupt.

Philosophically appealing as the theory might be, it is doubtful if it can ever be proven. What can be proven, however, is that Magdala existed right here, and archaeologists have uncovered enough of it to demonstrate that it was once an important, fortified town. Some think that Magdala was probably one of the most important towns in the area until Herod Antipas built Tiberias. As the new city grew with all its fine buildings and imperial name, wealthy, important, and powerful citizens likely moved there, and this left Magdala to inherit the destitute and the pathetic. It follows, then, that this would be a more important focus of Christian love and concern. Further excavations may reveal more evidence, and archaeologists may be able to eventually prove that the quality of life in Magdala degenerated once Tiberias was built.

If we can find a "tower" of will in the name Magdalene, we can find also very strong symbolism in the woman's given name. Jesus didn't know this woman as Mary — that's an anglicized version of her Hebrew name — Miriam — and Miriam stems from a Hebrew verb meaning defiant. Somehow, it is all symbolically appropriate.

Another four miles up the coast we come to a broad plain, Biq'at Ginnosar — the Vale of Ginnosar or Gen. For the next five miles of coastline, the rolling Galilean hills flatten into a level and productive agricultural belt, well watered with streams trickling down from the mountains. Most Catholic scholars identify this as the Land of Gennesaret of the Gospels, the place of miracles: ". . . he came down with them [the apostles] and stood on a level place, with a great crowd of his disciples and a great multitude of people from all Judea and Jerusalem and the seacoast of Tyre and Sidon, who came to hear him and to be healed of their diseases; and those who were troubled with unclean spirits were cured. And all the crowd sought to touch him, for power came forth from him and healed them all" (Lk 6:17-19).

This is that "level place," there can be no doubt. Indeed, there is no other level ground large enough to accommodate the thousands who came from all around the country to follow Jesus. St. Mark, however, even gives us a name for this place of miracles: "And when they had crossed over, they came to land at Gennesaret, and moored to the shore. And when they got out of the boat, immediately the people recognized him, and ran about the whole neighborhood and began to bring sick people on their pallets to any place where they heard he was. And wherever he came, in villages, cities, or country, they laid the sick in the market places, and besought him that they might touch even the fringe of his garment; and as many as touched it were made well" (Mk 6:53-56).

Such glorious days they must have been! We stand upon this open plain, with the Sea of Galilee to our east, and the mountains ringing round us on all other sides, and imagine the grand spectacle. How many thousands gathered here? Who were the now-nameless people who camped here, beside the brooks of Ammud, Zalmon, and Arbel, waiting hours, or perhaps days, or even weeks, just for a brief opportunity to hear His words, or to help a sick friend or relative touch the hem of His cloak? The Gospels tell us they traveled from Jerusalem, three or four days' journey from the south, and Phoenicia's coastal cities of Tyre and Sidon, an equal distance to the northwest, in what is now Lebanon. It is pleasing just to sit here, on this plain, and simply imagine the good feeling, the healing, the generosity, and the love that flowed through here. So often, historical landmarks are associated with great trials and suffering — here some brave men fought a battle; there other brave men risked their lives declaring independence, and over there occurred a tragic disaster. Even the joy of Bethlehem is marred by the historical fact of Herod's barbarisms and the Slaughter of the Innocents. But here, on the Plains of Ginnosar, there is only goodness.

Most of the plain today is occupied by a kibbutz, maintaining an attractive resort hotel on the beach. Kibbutz Ginnosar is well known for its excellent climate and fertile soils, which today produce great abundances of bananas, dates, vegetables, and other farm produce. And, of course, this settlement also has its own fishing enterprise.

A bit farther up the coast we come to Tabgha — the Seven Springs (Latin: *Septem Fontes* — Greek: *Heptapegon*). The crowds followed Jesus here, too, and it was here that He fed the five thousand followers with "the five loaves and the two fish" (Mk 6:41).

Tabgha is a remarkable pilgrim site because of the extraordinary restoration work going on here in recent years. Archaeologists have uncovered parts of a fourth-century sanctuary here, but it was not until the fifth century that a truly magnificent Byzantine "Church of the Multiplication of the

Loaves and Fishes" was built here at the site of the miracle.

That elegant church stood for only two centuries and was destroyed in A.D. 636 when Muslim Arab armies conquered this part of the Holy Land and set about obliterating all traces of Christian and Jewish belief.

The foundations of the church lay buried beneath its own rubble for nearly thirteen centuries. In 1911, archaeologists began probing in that rubble and discovered some beautiful mosaics. Then, through the 1930s, a full-scale project excavated the entire site, revealing much of the splendor of the Christian empire.

Until 1967, this site was in Israel, but so close to the Syrian-controlled Golan Heights that few people were interested in doing much more than visiting the ruins of Byzantine culture and faith. But with the Israeli victory in the 1967 Six-Day War, the Syrians were pushed beyond the Golan, and the region around the Sea of Galilee became much safer. And then people started thinking about building a new church.

The new church was to be something special. The Benedictine monks tending the site found some backing from the German Association of the Holy Land, plus the technical cooperation of restoration experts at the Israel Museum, and help from various Israeli government officials. Together they built a new church. And today, Tabgha has the world's only fully rebuilt Byzantine church.

The building was consecrated on Sunday, May 23, 1982, a balmy day along the shores of the Sea of Galilee. It was a day when Cardinal Joseph Hoffner, the Archbishop of Cologne, came to see what German Catholics had raised funds to build, a day when Jewish restoration professionals and Israeli officials came to turn over their efforts to the new Catholic church, a day when thousands of pilgrims gathered around the magnificent building and listened to the speeches and sermons and pealing of bells.

The entire church follows the classical Byzantine plan. Before entering the church, one must pass through an atrium — a peaceful garden with a blossoming mimosa tree in it. Beneath the tree is a seven-spouted fountain. Surrounding this atrium is a graceful cloister.

Father Bargil Pixner, O.S.B., who has been connected with the construction and archaeological work for years, says the Byzantine atrium formed a useful transition zone. "Crossing this threshold from the busy world outside, the people would prepare themselves here, in the coolness and quiet, to enter the sanctuary for prayer."

The interior of the stone church is remarkably austere. Clean lines are shaped by high, soaring arches and by massive, unadorned stone columns. Its classical basilica architecture, with traditional towers, nave, apses, and high altar, is covered by a cruciform, red-tiled roof. It looks precisely the same as the great church that was built here fifteen centuries ago.

Much of the ancient church has been incorporated into the new basilica. The new house of worship stands on the ancient foundations, assuring that the ancient architecture and dimensions have been kept. And some of the loveliest mosaic artistry of Constantine's Christian empire have been preserved in the floor. The mosaic spreads across five thousand square feet and depicts a broad variety of natural subjects, including various species of birds and plants. Other motifs in the mosaic include extensive geometric patterns and two Greek inscriptions.

When archaeologists excavated the site, they found about half of this marvelous mosaic was either destroyed or missing. The Benedictines called in experts from the Israel Museum and, over several years, the entire mosaic floor has been restored. Led by Dodo Shenhav, chief of the museum's modern restoration laboratory, the experts painstakingly restored each fragment of the original mosaic. And where no pieces survived, the restorers made new pieces by cutting pieces of stone with hand tools.

"We want to make a clear distinction between the old and the new," Shenhav explained. "You will notice that the new mosaic additions echo only the design of the original — not the colors. Instead of the reds, yellows, and browns, we use only white, gray, and black. And to make absolutely sure that future researchers won't get confused, we have placed tiny metal tags inscribed with the date along the joint between the antique and modern mosaics."

There are more than a million pieces of mosaic stone in this floor, each set into place. It is easy to distinguish between the colorful original mosaic and the modern restoration. But the work is all tastefully done. Ancient designs and patterns have been filled in to give the overall appearance of unity.

The most important area of the mosaic is part of the original floor. It's located right in front of the altar and depicts a basket with five loaves of bread flanked by two fishes. The museum staff restored the original stones and set them into place. Today, they are part of the floor of an active, living church, in daily use as a house of worship.

We stroll through the church and realize something of Byzantine culture. For years, we've heard of Byzantine intrigues, oriental despotism, and proclivity for ornate architecture, and much of this has tarnished the image of the earth's first Christian realm. But now, with the reconstruction of the church at Tabgha, we can see another perspective of Byzantine life. And in the classical lines of this Byzantine church, we can see the origins of many other church buildings around the world, from simple American wood-frame churches to the glorious cathedrals of Europe. There is a uniting thread of architecture and of faith.

And outside, we wander near the shores of the Sea of Galilee. Despite the marvelous achievements in the reconstruction of this great church, we realize also that when the five thousand came to listen to Jesus, they had no church. Rather, they sat out in the open, upon the architecture of the Creator, to listen to the teachings of the Son.

Non Sum Dignus •
Town of the Centurion:
Capharnaum, and Beyond

BLIND DISCIPLINE was the key to Rome's success. Roman soldiers obeyed orders explicitly, without question. They were human automatons, serving in robotlike fashion.

The strict discipline forged an army that conquered the entire civilized world two thousand years ago. It was a relatively new concept at that time. But with this type of organization, Roman units could be bound with singular purpose and directed by a single man. When they were brought against opponents of even three or four times their size, their unified command almost always assured them of victory.

Roman discipline destroyed Carthage. It subdued the disorganized Greek city-states. It extended Roman authority from Britain to the Orient in the largest empire ever to exist. Understanding the key to Roman military success is important in understanding the Gospel story about Jesus and the Roman centurion, and appreciating the events which occurred here at Capharnaum, or Capernaum, an ancient fishing village on the north shore of the Sea of Galilee.

Most students of history and Scripture know that the legion was the essential organization of the Roman army. This was a unit of about five thousand soldiers, with auxiliary units such as calvary and administrators. Ten cohorts, each of about five hundred soldiers, formed the legion. The commanders of the legions and cohorts were "high brass" in modern military slang. They were a military aristocracy, usually from wealthy and influential Roman families, and often as much interested in politics as in soldiering.

The cohort was divided into five centuries, each with a hundred soldiers, commanded by a centurion. This officer was the pivot of the entire Roman army. The centurion was the on-the-scene officer-in-charge. His superiors were usually some distance away and sent their commands via messengers. His subordinates were the common soldiers, right at hand. His orders were face-to-face and verbal. The centurion was the vital link between the thinking command structure and the disciplined soldier. His was the command that actually put soldiers into battle. He was the officer who could order executions on the spot, with neither trial nor appeal. Any soldier who disobeyed his centurion could be condemned to death.

During battles, Roman centuries formed battle squares, and in the center of these squares stood the centurion. In essence, the soldiers fought to protect their centurion and to execute his commands. Thus, this officer was immediate, direct, and absolute. Roman centurions could give orders to soldiers that meant certain death, yet these orders were carried out and desertion was rare. Discipline reigned, and Rome conquered the greatest civilizations of antiquity.

It may seem like a long step between these battle-hardened veterans and receiving Communion in your parish church. But it isn't.

Every time you recite, "Lord, I am not worthy to receive you, but only say the word and I shall be healed," you are echoing the words of the centurion of Capharnaum, the first non-Jewish convert to Christianity.

The Gospels tell us that one day, after preaching to His followers, Jesus "entered Capernaum. Now a centurion had a slave who was dear to him, who was sick and at the point of death. When he heard of Jesus, he sent to him elders of the Jews, asking him to come and heal his slave. And when they came to Jesus, they besought him earnestly, saying, 'He is worthy to have you do this for him, for he loves our nation, and he built us our synagogue.' And Jesus went up with them. When he was not far from the house, the centurion sent friends to him, saying to him, 'Lord, do not trouble yourself, for I am not worthy to have you come under my roof; therefore I did not presume to come to you. But say the word, and let my servant be healed' " (Lk 7:1-7).

Jesus praised the centurion for his faith, and the servant was cured.

Certainly, we repeat a semblance of the centurion's words at Communion, but there are other nuances of this story that we might also consider. One thought is, of all the people in Capharnaum, the centurion was the most likely to make such a statement of faith. In his military career, the simple statement of an order virtually guaranteed it would be done. If the cohort commander gave the centurion an order, that commander didn't have to follow the centurion around. He had faith that his subordinate would do precisely what he was told. And the centurion knew if he gave an order to a common soldier, he wouldn't have to follow that soldier to make sure the1 order was carried out. Again, there was a matter of faith and trusting the subordinate to execute the order.

Thus, when the centurion gained faith in Jesus, he realized that Jesus' miraculous orders were enough to cure his servant. Jesus didn't have to "check up" on the functioning of nature and the cure of the servant. The simple spiritual command of Jesus was enough to heal the unseen servant, and the centurion knew this.

St. Luke reminds us that this centurion was particularly benevolent. During the time of Jesus, there was frequent strife between the Holy Land's Jewish population and the occupying Roman army. But there were occasional oases of peace. And Capharnaum was one such place.

Archaeological excavations of Capharnaum, led by Franciscan scholars Fathers Virgilio Corbo and Stanislao Loffreda, have revealed much of this fishing village that became so closely associated with the life of Jesus. When we meet with Father Corbo among the black basalt ruins, the priest tells us that first it's vital to understand the village's strategic location1. To the south is the Sea of Galilee, and to the north are the mountains of the Upper Galilee. Capharnaum itself is located on the coastal plain between the two. For thousands of years, this coastal plain formed the important pass for the *Vlia Maris* — the ancient highway from Egypt to Mesopotamia. Thus,

Capharnaum might have been only a simple fishing village, but it was built beside one of the most important highways of antiquity. Also important is the fact that it stood at the eastern end of the Galilee — a few miles east of here one entered the Province of Gaulanitis.

Thus, Father Corbo notes, Capharnaum was a border town on an extremely important highway, and t1 his meant that it saw lots of traffic and therefore lots of exposure to the ideas of the outside world. Being a border town, it was also a place for collecting customs taxes, and Gospel readers will recall that St. Matthew himself was a customs official before he became a disciple of Jesus. And, Father Corbo adds, where taxes are collected, one also finds soldiers to protect the treasury and assure safety for the merchants — therefore the centurion and his hundred soldiers.

The Franciscan archaeologists have uncovered several blocks of the ancient village. The main streets were paved with that same hard black stone which was used for building all the houses. Most houses were actually small compounds, and not residential buildings as we commonly think of them today. Instead, each compound had several one- or two-room buildings facing to a small central courtyard area. This arrangement, Father Corbo believes, provided for extended family residences, and two or three generations could be living together in the same compound. We know, for example, that St. Peter lived with his mother-in-law.

Five of the twelve apostles came from this small village, and Jesus spent much of His Galilean ministry here. Perhaps a thousand Jewish inhabitants lived here, too.

The Franciscan archaeologists are constantly developing new details and insights into the history of Capharnaum. It illuminates the Gospels, they say; it helps us to better understand the Holy Writ. "For example," Father Loffreda says, "We all know the parable about the lost coin [see Lk 15:8-10] and the difficulty of finding it, even in one of these tiny houses. But working here, one realizes that it is not like a modern house at all, with smooth floors and large windows. These houses of Capharnaum had very rough floors and tiny windows. It was dark inside them, and very difficult to find a coin dropped on such a floor. So, when we work among these buildings, such a parable becomes more alive to us, more meaningful.

"Working here," he continues, "we can feel the Gospels with our hands. We can see many things in the same perspective as the disciples; we can appreciate the many everyday references of the Gospels."

One of the most spectacular finds of Capharnaum is the remains of the village's synagogue. The Franciscan priests are certain that this is the building which the centurion built for the community. They are certain that this was the building where Jesus preached.

These remains are beneath the remains of a later, fourth-century synagogue. This later building is a piece of fine craftsmanship, and this indicates that, at the time it was built, the ruling Byzantine Christians must have been on relatively good terms with the Galilean Jews and there was religious toleration. Like so many other buildings in this region, however, that fourth-century synagogue was built on earlier foundations, and very careful excavations over the past decade reveal that those foundations date from the time of Jesus.

Thus, today it is possible for a pilgrim to visit Capharnaum and actually touch the remains of the synagogue where Jesus preached His "good news." This is the building of the Gospels: "And they went into Capernaum; and immediately on the sabbath he [Jesus] entered the synagogue and taught. And they were astonished at his teaching, for he taught them as one who had authority, and not as the scribes. . . . And they were all amazed, so that they questioned among themselves, saying, 'What is this? A new teaching! With authority he commands. . . ?' And at once his fame spread everywhere throughout all the surrounding region of Galilee" (Mk 1:21-22, 27-28).

The Franciscan excavations of the synagogue have yielded plenty of evidence — pottery shards positively identified from the time of Jesus, Roman coins that were in circulation at that time, and various other artifacts which all corroborate the claim that this was the synagogue where Jesus taught. "We have checked it and rechecked it," Father Loffreda says. "There can be no doubt."

One of the interesting finds here was a series of scratched incisions in the stones outside the synagogue. The Franciscan archaeologists believe that these scratches represent the "playing board" of an ancient game known as Nine Man Morris. Similar scratchings have also been found in the courtyard of the Antonia, the Roman fortress in Jerusalem, and archaeologists suspect that this game might have been a popular pastime for soldiers.

We look at the scratches and think of a balmy spring day nearly two thousand years ago. Jesus was preaching in this synagogue, just as He did on several occasions, and among the congregation listening to the sermon was the Roman centurion. The soldier was there because of his faith in Jesus, and because Jesus' miracle had cured his servant. The soldier was there, also, because he had built the house of worship as a gesture of friendship to the resident Jewish community. Also in the congregation of this large building — it measured about seventy by sixty feet — were St. Peter, St. Andrew, and perhaps a few other apostles.

The centurion, however, had to be in constant contact with his soldiers. If he sat in the synagogue for a sermon, it is likely that he left one or two runners waiting outside in case an emergency developed. And it's likely that the runners, with little to do but wait for their centurion, scratched the lines of their popular Nine Man Morris into the stone to while away the hours during which their officer remained inside.

Capharnaum was already an old community at the time of Jesus. The name as we know it from the Gospels is actually a Latinized corruption of K'far Nahum, the Village of Nahum, and it is believed that the Prophet Nahum once lived here, and is buried somewhere in the area.

The biblical Book of Nahum is a relatively short text,

written as poetry, prophesying the destruction of the Assyrian capital of Nineveh, which occurred in the year 612 B.C.

All through the centuries of its existence, the Franciscans have learned, life in this village was difficult. "I know and respect the sanctity of the church, the candles, and incense," Father Loffreda observes. "But there is also another approach. I have these feelings at Capharnaum. At work, sometimes, in the summer, it is so hot you cannot pick up the stones. I have burned my hands simply by touching the crowbar. I have learned that the incense of the first Christians was perspiration. Their life was rough, harsh."

After a short pause he says, "When I am at work in Capharnaum, I get a special feeling inside me. Feelings that I will never forget, never. As I told you, working here, we can feel the Gospels with our hands."

Jesus spent much time in Capharnaum. He taught here, and performed miracles here. Five apostles came from Capharnaum. No community so small was ever so favored. Yet, the Jews of Capharnaum did not follow Christianity. Indeed, four centuries later, they built a magnificent synagogue here.

Jesus knew these fisherfolk would not follow Him, and for this He cursed them: "And you, Capernaum, will you be exalted to heaven? You shall be brought down to Hades. For if the mighty works done in you had been done in Sodom, it would have remained until this day. But I tell you that it shall be more tolerable on the day of judgment for the land of Sodom than for you" (Mt 11:23-24).

Capharnaum survived as a simple village for another six centuries, until the Muslim Arab invasions, and was then swept into oblivion. The site was purchased by the Franciscans in 1894, and modest excavations were then started. But it was not until recent decades, with the work of Fathers Corbo and Loffreda, that truly substantive work was done. And thanks to their labors, today's pilgrims — like no others before — can walk into the center of this community, see the very streets where the apostles learned devotion, and touch the ancient stones of the synogogue where Jesus himself preached.

There is no need to send archaeologists to the next site we visit, for there were no buildings here during the time of Jesus. Due north of Capharnaum, just east of the road that leads into the Upper Galilee, is the grass- and rock-covered Mount of the Beatitudes. Here, Jesus preached one of the most beautiful sermons of all time — the Sermon on the Mount.

There is a small church and convent on the summit, and these belong to Italian Franciscan nuns. Set into the floor at the entrance of the church is the inscription "A.D. MCMXXXVII — 1937. XV Italica Gens." That second date means the fifteenth year of the Italian people — that is, fifteen years after Benito Mussolini seized power. The shrine was built with the support of the Fascist government in Italy, which, at the time, was trying to buy the favor of the Catholic Church.

Of interest inside the church are the symbols of the seven virtues inscribed into the pavement around the altar: Justice, Charity, Prudence, Faith, Fortitude, Hope, and Temperance.

But greater interest lies outside the church, for if in Capharnaum Jesus preached in the synagogue, here upon this mount Jesus preached outdoors, in the open, with the magnificent landscape of the Galilee spread all around. To the south, we can see the Sea of Galilee, with all its coastal communities — Tiberias, Magdala, Ginnosar, and the others. To the west are the rolling hills of the Galilee rising up toward Cana and Nazareth and out toward the Mediterranean. To the east are the Golan Heights, rugged and forbidding. And to the north are the Upper Galilee and the snow-capped peak of Mount Hermon.

It is a perfect day in late spring. The air is warm and sweet. The meadows here are carpeted with grasses, wildflowers, and many stones. We find a large rock, away from the other pilgrims visiting this hilltop, and sit on it. The Sea of Galilee is spread before us. There is a light breeze coming from the right, and it carries with it the fragrances of springtime.

We have but one purpose here. We want to reread the Ser-

The Holy Land

mon on the Mount at the place where Jesus preached it. It is a lovely episode that embraces three full chapters of the Gospels:

"Seeing the crowds, he went up on the mountain, and when he sat down, his disciples came to him. And he opened his mouth and taught them, saying:

'Blessed are the poor in spirit, for theirs is the kingdom of heaven.

'Blessed are those who mourn, for they shall be comforted.

'Blessed are the meek, for they shall inherit the earth.

'Blessed are those who hunger and thirst for righteousness, for they shall be satisfied.

'Blessed are the merciful, for they shall obtain mercy.

'Blessed are the pure in heart, for they shall see God.

'Blessed are the peacemakers, for they shall be called sons of God.

'Blessed are those who are persecuted for righteousness' sake, for theirs is the kingdom of heaven' " (Mt 5:1-10).

The Sermon continues with wondrous passages. Jesus encourages His disciples, telling them to let their good works be known. Jesus also confirms the Old Testament — the Commandments and the Prophets — and extends them. It is not enough to merely forbid killing, Jesus says, but we must go further and extend love to our enemies. Marriage cannot be dissolved by human courts. Truth must reign, and therefore there is no need for oaths: "Let what you say be simply 'Yes' or 'No'; anything more than this comes from evil" (5:37).

Christians must step beyond simple "eye-for-an-eye" justice and break the evil chain of retribution with love and generosity.

And there is even a little humor to be read, for Jesus tells us to love our enemies and pray for those who persecute us, "even the tax collectors." Few people spend much time praying for tax collectors these days. And probably less so then, because at that time the tax collectors were officials representing the Roman occupation forces, and little of the tax money remained in the Holy Land for civic improvements. Instead, it went to Rome for the imperial treasury. But we shall pray for the tax collectors all the same, including our favorite, St. Matthew, who wrote this very Gospel.

Upon this Galilean hilltop, Jesus taught us the value of anonymous charity and private prayer. And He taught us, right here, how to pray:

"Our Father who art in heaven,
Hallowed be thy name.
Thy kingdom come,
Thy will be done,
    On earth as it is in heaven.
Give us this day our daily bread;
And forgive us our debts,
    As we also have forgiven our debtors;
And lead us not into temptation,
    But deliver us from evil" (Mt 6:9-13).

Fasting, too, should be done in secret. The treasures of the soul are much greater than earthly possessions, and "You cannot serve God and mammon" (6:24).

Jesus gives us a little nature-appreciation lecture. "Look at the birds of the air. . . . Consider the lilies of the field, how they grow; they neither toil nor spin; yet I tell you, even Solomon in all his glory was not arrayed like one of these" (6:26, 28-29). And we look around us. Indeed, the beauty of nature is magnificent. And we can't help but think that Jesus had a purpose for bringing His disciples up to this open space for this most important sermon. He wanted them to be immersed in the beauty of nature, to be surrounded by the architecture of the Creator. And we sense there is a greater need to be more protective of this divine architecture. Those lilies Jesus spoke of are today an endangered species.

This is not a mere figure of speech. The Holy Land's native lily is commonly known as the Madonna lily. Scientists know the species as *Lilium candidum*. Its ancient Hebrew name is *shoshan halavan* — the white lily. Through the centuries, Christian pilgrims to the Holy Land did more than consider the lilies; they picked them! And today they are extremely rare. They are seen no longer on the Mount of the

Beatitudes. There are a few nature reserves in the region, however, where these lovely blossoms are carefully protected by Israeli nature wardens. Anyone caught picking these flowers is arrested and taken to a judge.

I fear, however, that we may be accused of doing much more than picking wildflowers. There was a time when even the magnificent King Solomon, the wealthiest of monarchs, could not hope to match the brilliance of God's creation. And this is still true in many places. But in many other places, it is not. For those pursuing wealth have polluted streams and fouled the air, and killed wild animals for pure pleasure, not need.

And I recall a thought of Joseph Wood Krutch, a great American naturalist: "When a man wantonly destroys the works of another man, we call him a vandal. But when a man wantonly destroys the works of the Creator, we call him a 'sportsman.' "

Forgive me, dear reader, for taking this momentary tangent from the Sermon itself. But the protection of nature is both my profession and an expression of my faith. This planet and its rich abundance are a gift of God. We have an ethical and religious responsibility to use this divine gift wisely, and to preserve it for all generations to come. And in my mind, polluting, sport hunting, and other destructions of the natural environment are sinful. We can show respect for our Creator by showing respect for His Creation.

Upon this mount, Jesus taught us to reserve our judgments and to avoid profaning sacred things. He tells us to pray, to ask, and to "treat others as you would like them to treat you." We are advised to follow the "straight and narrow" and to beware of false prophets. And we learn that the way to the kingdom of heaven is open to the person "who does the will of my Father who is in heaven" (cf. 7:1-21).

There is so much in these few pages of the Gospel. They are flowing with goodness, wisdom, and spirit. We read through them again and again.

In our Bible, the Sermon on the Mount covers a handful

of pages. Is there in all the world another few pages with so much good guidance?

We stand, stretch, and simply wander around these meadows thinking of the Sermon on the Mount.

According to tradition, Jesus prayed upon this mount, and it was here that He chose the twelve apostles and organized them into the nucleus of His Church: "In these days he went out into the hills to pray; and all night he continued in prayer to God. And when it was day, he called his disciples, and chose from them twelve, whom he named apostles; Simon, whom he named Peter, and Andrew his brother, and James and John, and Philip, and Bartholomew, and Matthew, and Thomas, and James the son of Alphaeus, and Simon who was called the Zealot, and Judas son of James, and Judas Iscariot, who became a traitor" (Lk 6:12-16). It was here that the Church was founded.

There is a good feeling as we descend from the Mount of Beatitudes and drive eastward along the northern shore of the Sea of Galilee. We cross some rolling countryside and then descend to a small bridge which crosses the River Jordan just a few hundred yards before it spills into the Sea of Galilee. It is a small river, and in many places it is lost among tall reeds and mudflats. Up on the eastern bank we are in the foothills of the Golan, former Syrian territory. Less than a mile from the bridge is a left turn-off, and within minutes we enter the ruins of Bethsaida-Julias.

The excavation work here still has very far to go, and today the site is not very impressive at all. But its importance in the Gospels was enormous. The apostles Peter and Andrew were born here, and it was also the home of Philip. Jesus worked here, preached here, performed miracles here: ". . . they came to Bethsaida. And some people brought to him a blind man and begged him to touch him. . . . Then again he laid his hands upon his [the man's] eyes; and he looked intently and was restored. . ." (Mk 8:22, 25-26).

It was here that the second feeding of the multitudes took place: "And he took them and withdrew apart to a city called

Bethsaida. When the crowds learned it, they followed him; and he welcomed them and spoke to them of the kingdom of God, and cured those who had need of healing." The story continues, telling us that in the late afternoon the apostles advised Jesus to send the people away to find food and a place to sleep, for they did not have enough food to offer the five thousand people. There were but five loaves of bread and two fish. Taking these bits of food, Jesus "looked up to heaven, and blessed and broke them, and gave them to the disciples to set before the crowd. And all ate and were satisfied, and they took up what was left over, twelve baskets of broken pieces" (cf. Lk 9:10-17).

Indeed, after Jerusalem and Capharnaum, Bethsaida is the most frequently mentioned community of the Gospels; yet until very recently its precise location had been lost in the rubble of war. Benedictine Father Bargil Pixner must be credited with much of the work identifying this ancient knoll as the Bethsaida of the Gospels. After extensive surveys of the region, and intense study of all historical sources, both in the Gospels and in secular literature, the Benedictine priest gradually narrowed down his investigation. Ancient Roman literature was very helpful, for from these texts Father Pixner learned that ancient Bethsaida was located in the territory of Philip the Tetrarch — east of the River Jordan — and that it had been elevated to the status of "polis" (or municipality) in the year 4 B.C. and had its name enlarged to Bethsaida-Julias to honor the daughter of Roman Emperor Augustus Caesar's daughter Julia.

Studying maps of the region, Father Pixner decided a small hill known as Et-Tell was a likely spot to search for this Gospel community. And on investigating the site, he found that some unintentional archaeological work had been conducted before his arrival. In the years 1948 to 1967, this had been the front line of the Syrian army, and they had dug trenches back and forth across the hill. After 1967, when the area became accessible, Father Pixner began probing in those old Syrian trenches and started turning up bits of pottery that have since been positively identified as coming from the time of Jesus.

There were a few other problems, however, and one of the trickiest knots was a report that Bethsaida-Julias was located on the beach of the Sea of Galilee. The site being explored by Father Pixner is nearly a mile from the water's edge. So the priest studied some geology and discovered that nearly all the land between the village and the sea is silt deposit. "The fact that Israeli engineers, trying to construct a permanent bridge over the Jordan to replace two provisional ones there, have failed to find any terra firma on which to erect the bridgeheads, argues for the alluvial composition of the terrain." Thus Father Pixner believes that the site was a lakefront village twenty centuries ago, but that over the past two thousand years, silt carried down by the Jordan River and deposited at its mouth collected there to create a delta which built a mile of land out into the sea.

Father Pixner adds more evidence. An ancient document says that Bethsaida-Julias was located close to the Jordan River. Ethnological reports describe Et-Tell as having been the main encampment of the Bedouin tribe of Tellawiyeh, which the priest believes may be a corruption of Tell-Julia.

But what he terms "most convincing" is the detailed battle reports of Josephus Flavius, who describes an incident during the revolt of A.D. 66, during which the Jewish rebel forces under Josephus fought the Roman loyalists under Sylla. The description of ravines, attack routes, escape paths, and distances from other communities fits perfectly with the Et-Tell site of Bethsaida-Julias.

Major excavation work still needs to be done, Father Pixner observes, but at least the site is now well protected, as it has been incorporated into a newly created Israeli national park.

For the time being, Father Pixner is campaigning for a modest improvement: "For the Benefit of Christian pilgrims, it would be appropriate to have a small area on top of Et-Tell set aside for the reading of pertinent Bible passages and for quiet meditation as a mark of respect for the birthplace of the Prince of the Apostles and his brother Andrew."

As his own contribution, Father Pixner has set up his own memorial stone, a large block of basalt with a number of symbols carved into it. Two eyes near the top commemorate the healing of the blind man, while the Hebrew inscription *"Netzer Yishai"* means a "shoot from the stump of Jesse" (Is 11:1), and from this grows a branch — which was a common Judeo-Christian symbol in this region. Beside this is a rainbow arcing over a numbered cross — each number symbolizing a covenant of God, the first being with Adam, Noah, and Abraham, the second with the twelve tribes, and the third being the Christian covenant.

Father Pixner is a well-known scholar in Israel today, and also a well-known worker and peacemaker. He's involved with Jerusalem's Ecumenical Circle of Friends in studies at archaeological sites like Bethsaida-Julias and the Via Dolorosa. He teaches German Catholic theological students at Beit Yosef in Jerusalem and at the Benedictine monastery at Tabgha. Among his most impressive finds were the remains of the ancient Essene Gate, one of the entry gates to Jerusalem at the time of Jesus. The site is located at the end of a Protestant cemetery on Mount Zion. Nearby, he believes, are the remains of the first Christian church in Jerusalem. Simeon bar Cleopha, a cousin of Jesus, fled to Pella in A.D. 66 to escape the Roman destruction of Jerusalem, he said. And on his return, in the year 75, he built a Judeo-Christian synagogue in the ruins of the city. Father Pixner is also involved with deciphering some of the Dead Sea Scrolls and publishes many articles in scholarly journals detailing his prolific theories on the early Church and the time of Jesus. Not all of his theories are accepted by all scholars — but then this remarkable priest has been known for many decades as an individualist and a rebel.

He got himself into some hot water forty-five years ago when, as a young man in his native Germany, he was drafted into the army and refused to take the oath of allegiance to Hitler. Argument drifted to the Sermon on the Mount. An

SS officer ridiculed Jesus' instructions to "love thy neighbor."

"I cannot hate anyone," the young Catholic replied. "The Jews are also my brothers."

Fortunately for the young Pixner, the Nazis soon lost the war. After study and ordination, he came to Israel and studied Hebrew at a Jewish *ulpan* (school for language), and after that, Father Pixner volunteered as a laborer at a kibbutz near Jerusalem.

In setting up the Ecumenical Circle of Friends, Father Pixner said that religious communities have been divided by two many barriers: "It seemed to me that a grass-roots movement was needed. It was unlikely that the ecclesiastical hierarchy would initiate anything. We needed to become friends."

There's one last site to visit in our itinerary for this chapter. We drive down the eastern shore of the Sea of Galilee, beneath the looming mass of the Golan Heights, to a place where a team of road workers recently discovered the ruins of a fifth-century Byzantine church and monastery. Archaeologists descended on the site like bees finding nectar. And they worked just as busily.

Exploring the area, they discovered a small chapel carved into the rock farther up a nearby slope. After two years of careful study, the archaeologists believe they have discovered the Gerasenes of the Gospel: "They came to the other side of the sea, to the country of the Gerasenes. And when he had come out of the boat, there met him out of the tombs a man with an unclean spirit, who lived among the tombs; and no one could bind him any more, even with a chain; for he had often been bound with fetters and chains, but the chains he wrenched apart, and the fetters he broke in pieces; and no one had the strength to subdue him. Night and day among the tombs and on the mountains he was always crying out and bruising himself with stones. And when he saw Jesus from afar, he ran and worshiped him; and crying out with a loud voice, he said, 'What have you to do with me, Jesus, Son of the Most High God? I adjure you by God, do not torm1ent me.' For he had said to him, 'Come out of the man, you unclean spirit!' And

Jesus asked him, 'What is your name?' He replied, 'My name is Legion; for we are many.' And he begged him eagerly not to send them out of the country. Now a great herd of swine was feeding there on the hillside; and they [the unclean spirits] begged him, 'Send us into the swine, let us enter them.' So he gave them leave. And the unclean spirits came out, and entered the swine; and the herd, numbering about two thousand, rushed down the steep bank into the sea, and were drowned in the sea. The herdsmen fled and told it in the city and in the country. And people came to see what it was that had happened. And they came to Jesus, and saw the demoniac sitting there, clothed and in his right mind, the man who had had the legion; and they were afraid. And those who had seen it told what had happened to the demoniac and to the swine. And they began to beg Jesus to depart from their neighborhood. And as he was getting into the boat, the man who had been possessed with demons begged him that he might be with him. But he refused, and said to him, 'Go home to your friends, and tell them how much the Lord has done for you, and how he has had mercy on you' " (Mk 5:1-19).

A fantastic story? There have been doubting Thomases. But now we can explore the site and find much of the physical description written into the Gospels. Only since the site's discovery in 1984 by that Israeli road crew have we been able to visit this extraordinary place and piece together more physical evidence that serves to illustrate and reveal the Gospels.

Today, we can walk among the pillars that have been re-erected at this site, and sit beside an ancient olive press. The Byzantine church has been excavated, and a lovely mosaic revealed. There is a side chapel, and near its entrance a stone trap door was discovered that opened a passage to a vaulted tomb. Forty-four skeletons were found within.

The entire area has been excavated by the Israel Department of Antiquities and restored by the Israel National Parks Authority, as a landscaped archaeological park.

The archaeological scholars date the small rock-carved chapel to shortly after the time of Jesus. Nearby are many caves, where the madman likely lived. The earth around them is littered with many sharp flints, and we can only recall St. Mark's report: "Night and day among the tombs and on the mountains he was always crying out, and bruising himself with stones" (5:5).

The steep, rock-cut path to the old chapel passes a wall marked with many crosses and symbolic branches — just like the one Father Pixner added to the monument at Bethsaida. Within the chapel, a stone column still stands.

The archaeologists believe that this chapel was the original shrine commemorating that miraculous healing, and this served the Christian community for several centuries until the Byzantines built their fifth-century church and monastery at the foot of the hill. Ancient church records reveal that Cyril of Scythopolis visited this shrine in A.D. 491, and that in the year 723 St. Willibald offered prayers here.

A short walk from here is a high cliff rising above the Sea of Galilee, a cliff that for uncounted centuries has been known as "*el-Kafze*" — "the place of the leaping." And now scholars are beginning to believe that this was not another "lover's leap" from a romantic tale, but rather could well have been the place where the two thousand pigs, having received the demoniac spirits of the madman, leaped to their deaths.

There are many more tales around the Sea of Galilee. There are archaeological discoveries at Chorazin and Almagor. There are mysteries still hidden in the depths of the sea. Archaeologists excavating the home of St. Peter in Capharnaum have discovered fishing hooks.

Day by day, the land and the sea are revealing more about the life and times of Jesus. A century ago, the famous American writer Mark Twain commented to his travelogue *Innocents Abroad* that Capharnaum "was only a shapeless ruin. It bore no semblance to a town and had nothing about it to suggest that it had ever been a town." Today, this can no longer be said. Capharnaum has been excavated and revealed. And all the pieces are fitting into place. For the first time in nearly two thousand years a pilgrim can come in face-to-face contact

The Holy Land

with the world of Jesus. We can rub our hands across rough black stone floors and understand how difficult it is to find a lost coin here. We can climb into the cliffs of the Gerasenes, where a madman howled and cut himself with sharp rocks. We can even find piles of sharp flint. And we can climb to the summit of the Mount of the Beatitudes to read the Sermon on the Mount and know, with certainty, these are the places made holy by the life of Jesus.

10 'Vade, Satanas!' •
From the Garden of Eden
to the Mount of Temptation

A MERE sixty miles could separate the Garden of Eden, where Satan successfully tempted Adam and Eve to eat from the tree of knowledge, from the Mount of Temptation, where Satan unsuccessfully tempted Jesus with earthly kingdoms. Both of these sites of temptation are apparently located near the Jordan River — Eden perhaps not far from the Sea of Galilee, and the Mount of Temptation not far from the Dead Sea.

Every few years, archaeologists find an older link to the Bible somewhere under the earth of Israel, but now it appears that they have dug clear back to the first chapter of Genesis. A team of archaeologists reported recently in the prestigious British science journal *Nature* that they have evidence that links their archaeological excavations at Ubeidiyeh with the Garden of Eden.

The Israelis, understandably, are quite enthusiastic about the discovery, albeit a bit skeptical, too. Kibbutzniks at the village of Afikim on whose land the archaeological site is located, have decorated the entrance to their settlement with gay, hand-painted signs that read "THIS WAY TO PARADISE." A more sober assessment is offered by Professor Ofer Bar Yosef, senior archaeologist at Hebrew University of Jerusalem, who has many seasons of work at the Ubeidiyeh site.

Professor Bar Yosef acknowledges that this is the most ancient excavated site in Israel, and probably the most ancient in all Asia. Outside his Jerusalem office is a glass showcase with artifacts from the site — animal bones and stone tools thought to be more than a million years old. But he thinks the Ubeidiyeh site is more of an allegorical Garden of Eden, for it represents the transition between two major phases in the early development of human civilization. The first phase, he explained, would be the Paleolithic (or Early Stone) Age, which could be understood as a Garden of Eden. People living at that time belonged to a hunting and gathering society that offered a leisurely and undemanding lifestyle. "Ubeidiyeh was one of the earlier sites of hunters and gatherers, and for those who lived there at the time, it represented a Garden of Eden," he said. This undemanding life continued until 8000 B.C., when the Neolithic (or New Stone) Age was ushered in by the agricultural revolution. People learned then how to plant and reap. Food supplies became much more stable because of agriculture, but this stability also required much work.

"This marked the start of a far more arduous way of life," Professor Bar Yosef said. "We know that this agricultural revolution began in the Near East. In the account of the expulsion of Adam and Eve from the Garden of Eden, we have what may be seen as a dramatization of this transition."

Jennie Goldman of the Israel Interfaith Association surveyed the stony, sun-baked hills at Ubeidiyeh. "A far cry from the traditional lush image of the Garden of Eden!" she observed. "However, if we were to travel back in time a million or so years, we would behold a very different scene. For excavations on the site have revealed that this area was once a lake fringed with forests of oak and pine, where horses, giraffes, hippopotamuses, and elephants roamed wild."

She went on to say: "It is all too clear that Paradise is not what it used to be!"

The claimed discovery of the Garden of Eden is a very popular topic of conversation among archaeologists and religious scholars in Israel today. But most tend to agree — bombastic claims of British archaeologists notwithstanding — the most that can be said for the Ubeidiyeh site is that it could be a symbolic Garden of Eden. They all agree, in a historical way, that most of humanity's civilizing influences and practices started in the Middle East, and perhaps right in this immediate area. Wild wheat and barley were planted by farmers here, as were many garden vegetables. Goats and sheep were domesticated by capturing wild animals and hand-taming them for generations and generations. Humanity began to build communities in this region, and Jericho, a bit more than an hour's drive southward, is today the oldest known city on earth.

Was the tree of knowledge the knowledge of agriculture, animal husbandry, and community building? Genesis tells us that the tree of knowledge revealed good and evil, but living in fixed communities creates the scene for good and evil. Before humanity adopted these ways, all the world was free and there was no concept of ownership. But once there were homes and fields and herds, there was something to own — and something to steal, motive for violence, motive for lies.

Organized societies created the first religions, too. But these were pagan worship. Certainly, the "civilizing" of humanity in the Neolithic Age — after people left the ways of Ubeidiyeh — made it possible for people to offend the Almighty and injure their fellow creatures. And it was not until Yahweh's Ten Commandments that people had a firm set of rules to guide them in their use of the fruits from the tree of knowledge.

We sit on these bare slopes and ponder. How close to Eden are we? How much more difficult was it for people of good will and intentions, thousands of years ago, who could not find guidance in the Commandments, or refuge in the knowledge of God. In the Garden of Eden, humans ate from the tree of knowledge of good and evil — and then, for thousands of years after that time our ancestors wandered in hopeless blindness, not knowing how to use this knowledge, with no awareness of redemption.

A twenty-minute drive to the west brings us to the peak of Mount Tabor. The road up this 1,840-foot mountain finds us following many switchback hairpin curves ascending through a lovely variety of natural vegetation. There are lush Tabor oak trees with their elongated acorns, and many types of bushes and wild flowers. Here one also finds wild barley, the ancient ancestor of our domestic barley.

At the top, we look around and find an astonishing view in all directions — the Sea of Galilee off to the northeast and Nazareth to the northwest. Broad and fertile valleys lie between many mountains. Off to the south we see Mount Gilboa, where King Saul and his son Jonathan were killed in battle with the Philistines. To the west is Carmel, where Elijah challenged the false prophets of Ba'al, and just south of it is Megiddo — biblical Armageddon — where Revelations says the forces of good and evil, understood by humanity since the Garden of Eden, will clash in the great struggle at the End of Days.

But standing right before us on this mountaintop is a fine Franciscan church, the Basilica of the Transfiguration. It is here, the Church tells us, that Jesus took Peter, James, and John, "and led them up a high mountain apart. And he was transfigured before them, and his face shone like the sun, and his garments became white as light. And behold, there appeared to them Moses and Elijah, talking with him. And Peter said to Jesus, 'Lord, it is well that we are here; if you wish, I will make three booths here, one for you and one for Moses and one for Elijah.' He was still speaking, when lo, a bright cloud overshadowed them, and a voice from the cloud said, 'This is my beloved Son, with whom I am well pleased; listen to him.' When the disciples heard this, they fell on their faces and were filled with awe. But Jesus came and touched them, saying, 'Rise, and have no fear.' And when they lifted up their eyes, they saw no one but Jesus only" (Mt 17:1-8).

It was here, upon this mountain, that these most favored apostles saw Jesus in all His glory. Here they saw Moses, the law-giver, and Elijah, the great prophet. Here, they heard the voice of the Almighty and the instructions to listen to Jesus.

Such a great and profound event occurred here, and it is so difficult to appreciate. What is the beauty of a wild lily or a colorful sunset compared to this? How profound is a simple prayer when matched against this? How can a simple layman understand the glory of the Transfiguration?

The church here is relatively modern, completed in 1923.

It's a fine edifice of light limestone in the Italian style. Like so many other churches of the Holy Land, archaeologists have probed its foundations and found remnants of the Crusaders and the Byzantines.

This great mountain has an illustrious history that predates the Transfiguration. The Book of Judges recalls a time, more than a thousand years before Jesus, when Deborah was a judge of Israel and the land had suffered under Canaanite oppression for twenty years. Deborah summoned Barak, the Israelite military leader, and together they joined their forces on the slopes of Mount Tabor. Sisera, the Canannite general, threw all his forces, including nine hundred iron chariots, against the Israelite army — "And the LORD routed Sisera and all his chariots and all his army before Barak at the edge of the sword; and Sisera alighted from his chariot and fled away on foot" (Judg 4:15).

After this battle, the Canaanites no longer posed a serious threat to the Israelites, nor could they impose taxes of tribute. It was a key event toward Israelite independence and the installation of David as king, founding the royal bloodline that would return to Mount Tabor ten centuries later in the Person of Jesus.

While it is most appropriate to read the Gospel according to St. Matthew upon the peak of Mount Tabor, and to ponder the profound mystery of the Transfiguration, it is also pleasant to reread Judges in the Old Testament, for this is the great Song of Deborah: "That the leaders took the lead in Israel, / that the people offered themselves willingly, / bless the LORD! / Hear, O kings; give ear, O princes; / to the LORD I will sing, / I will make melody to the LORD, the God of Israel" (5:2-3) It is a song of deliverance, a song of joy. Do you hear the rhythms and melodies that will mature more than ten centuries later when our Lady sings the Magnificat?

We follow a road back down the mountainside, across the valley, and up into the mountains of Samaria on our southward journey. After about thirty miles, we come to the ruins of Samaria or, as it was known at the time of Jesus, Sebaste.

The Holy Land

Here we have an entire ancient city excavated and open to the public, and it is possible for us to wander among these extensive ruins and consider a bit of its history.

When King Solomon died, his kingdom was divided between two sons, and the southern portion became the Kingdom of Judah whle the north was known as the Kingdom of Israel. Jerusalem remained the capital of the southern kingdom, but King Omri, in the year 887 B.C., founded Samaria as the capital of the northern kingdom.

Subsequently, the evil King Ahab embellished the city and, with his queen, the conniving Jezebel, opened the door to paganism and the worship of Ba'al. Great internal strife arose. A resistance movement, led by the great prophet Elijah, confronted Ahab in pitched struggles until the year 853 B.C., when Ahab died in battle against the Syrians. Vindication lasted slightly more than a century, for in 722 B.C., the Assyrian monarch Shalmaneser V attacked the city and, capturing it, reduced it to rubble. The survivors were carried away as slaves.

It was gradually rebuilt, and in 35 B.C. Herod undertook a major reconstruction project here and renamed it *Sebastos* (Sebaste), which is the Greek word for Augustus. The puppet king wanted to flatter his Roman boss. It was here that Herod had two sons, Alexander and Aristobulus, taken prisoner and strangled.

It was here also that the head of John the Baptist was buried. St. Mark tells us about a birthday party of Herod Antipas, surviving son and successor of Herod the Great. Herod Antipas had dismissed his wife in order to marry Herodias, the daughter of his half-brother Aristobulus (the one strangled by Herod) and the divorced wife of his other half-brother Herod Philip — and St. John challenged the king, telling him "it is not lawful for you to have your brother's wife." This angered Herodias, who wanted to kill St. John, but Herod Antipas was afraid to do more than have the Baptist arrested and held in chains. At the birthday party, Herodias's young daughter Salome danced for the king and so delighted him that he promised the girl anything she wanted. Salome ran to her mother and asked what she would like. Back to the king the young girl went and, at her mother's insistence, demanded the head of John the Baptist on a platter. And so Herod Antipas ordered the immediate execution of the son of Elizabeth and Zechariah, forerunner and cousin of Jesus (see Mk 6:17-29).

The Catholic church near these ruins is named in honor of the Baptist.

Among these somber ruins, one may stroll along ancient streets before scores of ancient columns standing as silent sentinels to sadness and evil. The remains of a palace, a theater, the hippodrome, and other great public buildings can be viewed, and all around the edge of the city grow groves of olive trees.

Ten miles farther south we come to the modern city of Nablus, an Arabic corruption of "Neapolis" (New City). This is the ancient city of Shechem — the homeland of the Samaritans. During antiquity, the Samaritans were a powerful nation, and they figure in several passages of the Gospels. But the last thousand years have been extremely difficult for them, and they have dwindled to about five hundred persons who share serious genetic problems.

According to the Samaritans themselves, they are the direct descendants of the Israelite tribes of Ephraim, Gad, and Manasseh. During the Assyrian conquests of 722 B.C. and the subsequent deportations of the citizens of the Kingdom of Israel, they say, many escaped their conqueror's roundups and remained on the land.

Biblical history is somewhat different. The Second Book of Kings tells us that "the king of Assyria brought people from Babylon, Cuthah, Avva, Hamath, and Sepharvaim, and placed them in the cities of Samaria instead of the people of Israel; and they took possession of Samaria, and dwelt in its cities" (17:24).

Thus started a conflict between the Jews and the Samaritans.

In the year 586 B.C. King Nebuchadnezzar of Babylon led his armies against the surviving southern Kingdom of Judah, destroying it along with its capital, Jerusalem. The citizens of Judah — the Jews — were led away to the Babylonian captivity. And from this came one of the most moving prayers of the Bible: "By the waters of Babylon, there we sat down and wept, / when we remembered Zion. / On the willows there / we hung up our lyres. / For there our captors / required of us songs, / and our tormentors, mirth, saying, / 'Sing us one of the songs of Zion!' / How shall we sing the LORD's song in a foreign land? / If I forget you, O Jerusalem, / let my right hand wither! / Let my tongue cleave to the roof of my mouth, / if I do not remember you, / if I do not set Jerusalem / above my high joy!" (Ps 137 [136]:1-6).

The Babylonian captivity lasted only forty-seven years, and in 539 B.C. Cyrus the Great led the Persian armies against Babylon and conquered it. Cyrus then liberated the captives, and some forty thousand Jews walked from what is present-day Iraq back home to Jerusalem to rebuild their country. When they arrived, they found the Samaritans firmly entrenched to the north of Jerusalem.

The Jews accused the Samaritans of usurping the lands of their brothers of the Kingdom of Israel. The Samaritans claimed they themselves were the descendents of the Kingdom of Israel. One did not believe the other. And the ill-feeling caused by this rift was still very much a part of life at the time of Jesus.

St. John tells us of a time when Jesus was traveling by this way and stopped to rest beside an ancient well during the noon hour: "There came a woman of Samaria to draw water. Jesus said to her, 'Give me a drink.' For his disciples had gone away into the city to buy food. The Samaritan woman said to him, 'How is it that you, a Jew, ask a drink of me, a woman of Samaria?' For Jews have no dealings with Samaritans" (see Jn 4:1-9).

There followed the great sermon about the "living waters" of eternal salvation, and He told the Samaritan woman her innermost secrets. But still she resisted. She recalled the ancient rivalry between Samaritans and Jews: "Our fathers worshiped on this mountain [Shechem's Mount Gerizim]; and you say that in Jerusalem [Temple Mount] is the place where men ought to worship" (Jn 4:20).

But to this Jesus replied with the prophecy of a universal — a Catholic — Church: "Woman, believe me, the hour is coming when neither on this mountain nor in Jerusalem will you worship the Father. You worship what you do not know; we worship what we know, for salvation is from the Jews. But the hour is coming, and now is, when the true worshipers will worship the Father in spirit and truth. . ." (Jn 4:21-23).

A pilgrim today can visit this ancient well, which is in a most extraordinary place. On the outskirts of Shechem there is a half-built church tended by the Greek Orthodox. It was being built earlier in this century by Russian Tsar Nicholas II. But Nicholas ran into a revolution, lost his throne, his bank account — and his life, for that matter. And work on the great church was stopped. It hasn't restarted. Instead, Greek Orthodox monks tend gardens where floors and pews should be. The main walls are all standing, but there is no roof. Near where the altar should be, a small shed covers a flight of steps that descend into the ground. At the foot of these steps is a small room with a tiny altar, many burning candles, icons, and a well. The Greek monk tells us that this is Jacob's Well, where Jesus talked with the Samaritan woman.

"It is in Genesis [33:18-19] that we read that Jacob came here to Shechem and pitched his tent outside the city, and purchased these fields from King Hamor for one hundred pieces of silver," Archimandrite Thaddius tells us. "And these lands were left to Joseph, the son of Jacob, who dug this well. Joseph himself is buried not far from here. You may take the cup and taste the waters of this well."

There is a silver cup standing on the edge of the well, but the bucket suspended beneath a hand crank is empty. "Go ahead!" the Greek monk tells us. "Crank it down and fill it with water." And we do this.

It is a very long way to the bottom — "exactly one hundred and five feet," we are told by the monk. "But didn't the Samaritan woman tell us 'the well is deep' [Jn 4:11]?" We crank the bucket back up, sloshing all the way and banging against the inside of the well a few times. But the effort is worth it. The waters of this well are very clear and cool.

After emerging from the subterranean well room, we drive across town to Haret es-Samira, the Samaritan Quarter, and meet with Jacob ben Uzi ha-Kohen, a Samaritan priest. The rift with the Jews has healed in recent decades, he tells us, and the Israeli government has been very helpful in subsidizing the repair of the community's synagogue.

Of great importance, he notes, is that the religious leaders of the Samaritans consider Jews close enough to them to permit intermarriage — and such weddings are the only ones they'll sanction outside their own community. The Samaritans accept only the Pentateuch — the first Five Books of the Bible — and reject the rest of Jewish Scripture, as well as the Christian Gospels.

The Samaritan priest escorts us to the tomb of Joseph, who is also venerated by this sect as a Patriarch. Samaritan Scriptures, just like the Old Testament held by the Catholic Church, reveals the sequence of events leading up to the Patriarch's burial here. "Joseph inherited this land from his father Jacob," the Samaritan tells us. "But Joseph could not enjoy it, because he was sold into slavery by his brothers, and taken down to Egypt. But then Joseph became a powerful and important man in Egypt, a trusted official of the pharaoh. Yet all through this time, his heart remained here in his ancient homeland. When he was a very old man, Joseph prophesied a return to the Promised Land, and he made his people take an oath that when they did return, they would carry his bones with them for proper burial in the land of his fathers [see Gen 50:25]. Scripture later records that Joseph's bones indeed were gathered together by Moses," the Samaritan priest says, "and those bones were carried out from Egypt during the Exodus [see Ex 13:19]."

The Book of Joshua, which is not accepted by the Samaritans, nevertheless confirms the claim of Joseph's final resting place: "The bones of Joseph which the people of Israel brought up from Egypt were buried at Shechem, in the portion of ground which Jacob bought from the sons of Hamor the father of Shechem for a hundred pieces of money; it became an inheritance of the descendants of Joseph" (24:32).

The tomb itself is a small building with a domed roof. It is in a quiet corner of town, with several towering trees growing around it. Two Israeli soldiers sit by its gate, ensuring free access to all religious beliefs — for Joseph is venerated by Christians, Jews, Muslims, and Samaritans as one of the great Patriarchs. As we arrive, there are two Orthodox Jews chanting prayers within the tomb, while a Muslim sits outside. "I prefer to wait a few minutes until they are done," he tells us. "I want to make my prayers alone."

The Gospels tell us of another incident between Jesus and the Samaritans, although the location of the incident has been lost to history. While walking toward Jerusalem somewhere in these mountains, Jesus came upon a Samaritan village, and He sent a few of His disciples into the village to "make ready for him; but the people would not receive him, because his face was set toward Jerusalem" (Lk 9:52-53). Jesus the Jew ran into anti-Semitism. Hostility between Jews and Samaritans at this time must have been so great that anyone going to Jewish Jerusalem simply wouldn't be welcomed to pass through a Samaritan village.

These incidents make the parable of the Good Samaritan all the more meaningful. In the Gospel according to St. Luke (10:29-37), we read the famous parable about a man (presumably Jewish) who was attacked by robbers, beaten, and left half dead by the roadside. A Jewish priest and a Levite (teacher) both ignored the victim's sufferings; but a Samaritan passing along this road took pity on the suffering man, tended his wounds, and brought him to an inn. People who should have brought aid, didn't; and the man one wouldn't expect to give aid, did.

With this, Jesus tells us that all humanity is our neighbor, including our political rivals, people of other faiths, and those who have spurned us and refused to let us enter their villages.

We visit the "Inn of the Good Samaritan" on the roadside east of Jerusalem. It's about halfway down from the Holy City to Jericho — each city is about a dozen miles away. According to Christian tradition, this is where the Good Samaritan brought the robbery victim — and it's likely that this tradition is accurate.

The "inn" is actually a caravansary, or *khan* in Hebrew, built on the southern side of the road in a barren desert area. Thick stone walls protect all sides, and a long stone building occupies the southern flank. The western half of this building has stalls built into it, and watering troughs for animals, as well as places to store hay and harnesses. The eastern half is apparently built for human habitation. The rooms are large and airy, and it's likely that people slept here barracks-style, with several travelers sharing the same room. There is also a smaller room, perhaps for the innkeeper and his family. A courtyard within the walls covers large cisterns built into the limestone bedrock — great water reservoirs that are vital for desert travelers.

During ancient times, slow-moving caravans spent the night in these protected caravansaries whenever possible. They kept good supplies of food and water, and they offered fortresslike protection against the robbers who abounded in the hills. This particular caravansary does not date from the time of Jesus. Indeed, its architecture and construction appear to date from the time of the Ottoman Empire — just a few hundred years ago. But it is the only known caravansary on the route between Jerusalem and Jericho. Quite probably, the inn where the Good Samaritan brought the injured traveler stood on this site, but it has been rebuilt several times during the past two thousand years.

It's unlikely that there were any other caravansaries along this route for several reasons: even in the best of times, the Jerusalem-to-Jericho traffic could support only a single caravansary; the bedrock beneath this structure is good, which is an important consideration when building protective walls or the always-critical water cisterns; and finally, signal fires lit here can be seen by watchmen atop the Mount of Olives, beside Jerusalem. In the event the caravansary was attacked, a signal for help could be made from this location, but once one proceeds another hunded yards or so toward Jericho, the traveler loses sight of Jerusalem altogether.

Walking around the caravansary, we find it easy to imagine the activity that went on here as traders brought spices, silks, and gemstones from the Orient to Jerusalem, or perhaps simple pilgrims rested here before finishing their journey to the Holy City. It was the last night's stop before reaching Jerusalem from the east, and so people traveling great distances were probably quite excited when they halted here. Through most of the year, the travelers and their camels and donkeys probably slept outside in the courtyard, beneath the brilliant desert sky. The buildings were most likely used to shade the animals during the blistering hot summer days, or shelter them from the rare chill winter rain. And the same thing probably went for people.

One curious aspect about the story of the Good Samaritan involves asking what a Samaritan was doing here in the first place. This caravansary, and indeed the entire Jericho-Jerusalem highway, lies in the Judean Desert — a strictly Jewish neighborhood during the time of Jesus. Samaritans were not welcomed here any more than Jews were welcomed in Samaria.

Also curious in this parable is the report that the Good Samaritan gave the innkeeper two *denarii* to tend the robbery victim. A denarius was an ancient Roman silver coin, and worth quite a bit more than a few nights' stay at a simple caravansary. In modern terms, it would be akin to trying to break a $100 bill at a newsstand.

This comment, however, calls to mind the words of Philip Guedalla, the biographer. Much of his biographical research of the "Iron Duke" of Wellington involved sifting through the

Duke's old expense bills. "Show me how a man spends his money," Guedella said, "and you will show me what kind of man he is."

About two miles beyond the Inn of the Good Samaritan, a small dirt track branches off to the left. It twists and turns down the mountainside, and at the bottom we come to a desert ravine — "Wadi Kelt." From here, we have a six- or seven-mile hike due east across some of the most spectacular desert scenery in the Holy Land. Wadi Kelt slices across the Judean Desert and, for most of the year, it is but a dry ravine. In late winter, however, it can be a swollen river flooding down from the kilometer-high mountains around Jerusalem.

Following the stream-bed, we come across a small tribe of Bedouin nomads coming the other way. A middle-aged man leads a camel heaped high with baggage. An elderly gentleman walks beside him. "*Salaam alikum*," we greet them in Arabic. They reply with the same phrase — "May peace be with you." Four women, covered in veils from head to toe, scurry to the far side of the camel to hide themselves from view.

Two girls, in their early teens and not so heavily veiled as the older women, lead two donkeys, which are also heaped with great bundles. And coming up behind them are three boys, running barefoot on the hard desert gravel. They are trying to keep about thirty goats together in a herd — although the goats have other ideas about the discipline of march and the youngsters must run back and forth around the ravine to gather strays.

They pass quietly, and go on their way with the same desert stoicism which must have marked life in these parts through all times. I don't doubt that Jesus must have walked down this ravine at some time during His ministry. Did He cross through here during His forty days in the desert? Likely so. Wadi Kelt has long been an important desert highway. The Romans built an aqueduct along the walls of the ravine, and this watercourse — much repaired and rebuilt — still exists today. The aqueduct was originally built to carry water from Ein Kelt (Kelt Spring), a desert oasis, down to the fields around Jericho. But since it has always been an open aqueduct, it also provides a constant supply of fresh water along every inch of the ravine's length — and there aren't many desert highways that can boast of this.

About five miles down the ravine, we walk past St. George's Monastery, a mid-desert residence for Greek Orthodox monks. The monastery is built into an imposing cliff. In this area, they have created a number of lovely gardens, tapping water from the aqueduct to irrigate vegetables, flowers, and palm trees. Farther along the route, we pass a series of small cells where the monks sometimes retire for seclusion and meditation.

We climb up from the basin of the ravine to its southern wall and follow an ancient footpath along the aqueduct. Another mile or so along this way, we look across to the facing wall of the ravine and see the nest of a Bonelli's eagle, with the female and two downy eaglets. The male must be off somewhere looking for supper. These eagles are among the most spectacular birds in the world, and quite rare, too. They're true eagles, and very large birds indeed. But, unlike most other eagles, they don't spend so much time soaring on their broad wings. Instead, they're very active flyers, energetically beating their wings and flying with spectacular aerobatics. Did Jesus see such eagles in this region?

Suddenly, without expecting it, we turn a corner and the green plains of Jericho spread before us. Jericho, the ancient of ancients, was thousands of years old when Joshua stood before its walls.

Archaeological excavations here have identified the remains of the biblical battle, for in the depths, at a layer corresponding to about the thirteenth century B.C., there is a seam of ash and rubble — a sign that the city was conquered, destroyed, and then left for centuries before reconstruction.

Being wise pilgrims, we've seen to it that our car is waiting for us at the mouth of Wadi Kelt. And from here we can drive two miles north to Quarantal — an Arabic corruption of the Latin *Mons Quarantana*, the Mount of the Forty. According to tradition, Jesus fasted upon this mountain during His forty days in the desert, and here He was tempted by the devil: "Then Jesus was led up by the Spirit into the wilderness to be tempted by the devil. And he fasted forty days and forty nights, and afterward he was hungry. And the tempter came and said to him, 'If you are the Son of God, command these stones to become loaves of bread.' But he answered, 'It is written, / "Man shall not live by bread alone, / but by every word that proceeds from the mouth of God."' / . . . Again, the devil took him to a very high mountain, and showed him all the kingdoms of the world and the glory of them; and he said to him, 'All these I will give you, if you will fall down and worship me.' Then Jesus said to him, 'Begone, Satan! for it is written, / "You shall worship the Lord your God / and him only shall you serve."' / Then the devil left him, and behold, angels came and ministered to him" (Mt 4:1-4, 8-11).

The first part of the climb is a steep but firm path, followed by steps carved into the rock. Walking up this part of the mountain is about as easy as walking up the stairs of a thirty-story building — then we come to a door. Pulling a chain outside rings a bell inside, and in a few moments a Greek Orthodox monk comes to admit us. This is the Greek Orthodox Monastery of the Temptation. We look at all the nice religious objects they have to show us, a pretty chapel carved into the rock of the mountain, a series of meditation cells, some icons, and a balcony with a lovely view. And when this visit is completed, we ask to exit via the back door. From here, we can continue up the mountain. The footpath is very steep, and along much of the way we must find handholds to help us keep our balance. The mountain is exposed to the desert sun, and it's very hot to the touch. Forty days and forty nights out here — a mere forty minutes is exhausting! Up we climb on the crumbly rock. There's not a sprig of vegetation anywhere around, nor a bit of shade.

High above the monastery we find a level spot and a place to sit. And truly, it appears as if "all the kingdoms of the world and their glory" are spread before us. Immediately before us is ancient Jericho, and just beyond is a ribbon of green — vegetation growing along the banks of the River Jordan. Beyond the river is modern Jordan, the ancient Kingdom of Moab, where Mount Nebo rises. It was there that Moses died after having led his people to the gateway of the Promised Land. Beyond the mountains are the great Arabian and Syrian deserts, and the lands of ancient Assyria, Persia, and Babylon. Down to the right is the Dead Sea, the lowest place on the face of the earth, and along its shores we can discern Qumran, where the Essenic sects at the time of Jesus were drafting the Dead Sea Scrolls. Northward, beyond the hills of Samaria and the Galilee, lies present-day Lebanon — ancient Phoenicia. Behind us, the mountains rise toward the west and the Land of Israel. And down, far beyond to the southwest, lies Egypt, the land of the pharaohs.

It was here that Jesus tested His own humanity by confronting the temptations of the devil. They were very human temptations — loaves of bread for a starving man, the prospect of great empires, wealth, and, worst of all, paganism. The devil's invitation to be worshiped was not merely the price to be paid for worldly riches and power. It was something more sinister. It was a temptation in itself.

There is a medieval legend about Faust, the man who sold his soul to the devil in exchange for knowledge and power. Many people see a relationship between this story and the devil's temptation of Jesus — but this misses a very important point. Sitting on this mountain, it all becomes very clear. Faust's deal with the devil was a simple sales contract — he exchanged this for that. The temptation of Jesus involved more. Faust merely sold his soul; Jesus was invited to worship the devil. Faust's sale was passive, but actual worship must be active.

The devil invited Jesus to break the First Commandment on this mountain, and tragically, this seems to be the easiest of all Commandments to break. Much of the Bible tells stories of prophets continually preaching to the people, warning them of the dangers of idolatry and paganism — from the golden calf in Sinai through the thousands of little personal idols and Ba'al groves and pagan temples raised throughout the land. Monotheism's conflict with pagan idolatry is an age-old struggle, expressed in the purest form right on this mountaintop.

We sit upon this barren mountain and consider — idolatry is still a very serious problem today. And it's getting worse. True, there aren't many people who keep little clay statues of Ba'al the Canaanite god, or Dagon the Philistine god, stashed in a hidden closet for secret worship services. But then, today idolatry has taken a new perspective.

It was on this mountain that Jesus recalled the First Commandment and told us: "You shall worship the Lord your God, and him only shall you serve." It is a phrase that needs repeating time and again, for we still have our little idols and pagan practices.

Recall that most idols were mere objects of convenience during antiquity. People kept them and "prayed" to them — asking favors mostly. Few idols received "pure" worship. Instead, it was "protect me from my violent neighbors" or "grant me health and wealth" or "bring rains so we can have a bountiful harvest" — gimme, gimme, gimme. Idolators don't love. They want. And they're willing to sacrifice to get what they want, even to the point of casting infants into the fires of Moloch. Thus, the source of idolatry is greed, and its expression is convenience.

The source and the expression are still with us. Only the shapes of the idols have changed. But anything in our lives that supplants the worship of God can be nothing less than pagan idolatry.

Idols and paganism are merely false techniques for avoiding reality. They can be found in alcoholism, drug addiction, or even addictions to relatively benign things — television, games, any distraction. The key is the addiction, and not necessarily its form. Any addiction that submerges our sense of reality or supplants our worship of God is pagan idolatry.

This is what Jesus faced upon this mountain. By worshiping the devil, he could have avoided all the agony that He knew lay ahead. He could have avoided the terrible responsibility of it all. Worshiping the devil — the ultimate paganism — would have been convenient.

But He faced this challenge by embracing the First Commandment.

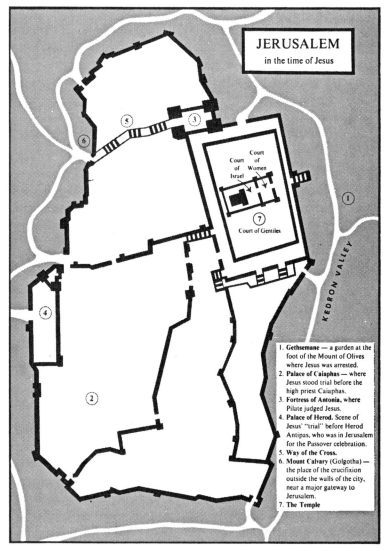

JERUSALEM
in the time of Jesus

Court of Israel

Court of Women

Court of Gentiles

KEDRON VALLEY

1. **Gethsemane** — a garden at the foot of the Mount of Olives where Jesus was arrested.
2. **Palace of Caiaphas** — where Jesus stood trial before the high priest Caiaphas.
3. **Fortress of Antonia,** where Pilate judged Jesus.
4. **Palace of Herod.** Scene of Jesus' "trial" before Herod Antipas, who was in Jerusalem for the Passover celebration.
5. **Way of the Cross.**
6. **Mount Calvary (Golgotha)** — the place of the crucifixion outside the walls of the city, near a major gateway to Jerusalem.
7. **The Temple**

The Holy Land

11 'Eamus in Judaeam' •
From the Jordan
to Jerusalem

ON OCTOBER 31, 1985, peace ruled a Middle Eastern front line. On that day, a Roman Catholic procession threaded its way between the guns of the Jordanian Arab Legion and the Israel Defense Forces to commemorate the baptism of Jesus at the site where this holy event occurred — in the River Jordan, about six miles southeast of the city of Jericho.

To understand the significance of the Catholic ceremony, we must turn the calendar back to 1948, when, with the approval of the United Nations, modern Israel was declared to exist.

It was immediately attacked by five Arab armies, one of which was the Arab Legion of a country then called Transjordan.

Until 1948, Transjordan (which means "across the Jordan") existed only east of the River Jordan. When Israel was created, Transjordan's Arab Legion joined the attack and crossed to the west bank of the river in an effort to crush the infant state of Israel.

The Arab attacks failed, but the actual borders of modern Israel were never really defined. Instead, there followed a series of "cease-fire lines," which marked the farthest incursion of each army once a truce was arranged. International agreements recognized that the final borders of countries in the region would be decided at an international peace conference — a meeting that has not yet taken place, except between Egypt and Israel.

With the cease-fire of 1948, Transjordan's Arab Legion had occupied some of the lands west of the River Jordan. Two years later, King Abdullah formally absorbed those lands into his kingdom and changed the name of his country from Transjordan to Jordan. The international community never recognized Jordan's claim to the "West Bank."

In June 1967, Egypt, Syria, and Jordan allied themselves for a new attack against Israel. In the central sector, Jordan threw the first stone and launched an assault against Israel. Israel responded furiously and hurled the Jordanian troops out of the West Bank region and back across the River Jordan. Today, Israel occupies this region, but has dropped the Jordanian term "West Bank," and now calls the territories by their ancient biblical names — Judea and Samaria. Israel has not absorbed these territories into its national sovereignty, although it has permitted Jews who wish to live there to do so, and new Jewish settlements in these regions have become a matter of international controversy.

Since 1967, the River Jordan has, along much of its length, formed the cease-fire line between Jordanian and Israeli troops. The bed of this modest stream, which is only about twenty-five to thirty feet across, is a rather wet "no man's land."

For centuries, many Christian communities — Roman Catholics, Greek Orthodox, Armenians, and others — maintained churches, monasteries, and shrines very close to the river along its western bank. From here, they conducted services in the river to commemorate the baptism of Jesus. Often, these ceremonies became very elaborate, with a great amount of symbolism and with thousands of pilgrims coming to participate.

But after 1967, it all changed. The war ended with a cease-fire, but not a peace. And within months, the river became a favored route for terrorist infiltration. Typically, PLO gunmen slipped into the river under the cover of night from the Jordanian side, and then emerged a few minutes later in the thickets on the Israeli side. Although their main intentions were to spread terror and death in Israel, the vast majority of these terrorists never got very far and were either captured or shot in gun battles with the Israel Defense Forces. A few, unfortunately, did manage to infiltrate into Israel.

The first buildings terrorists found upon crossing into the Israeli zone were the several Christian centers preserving shrines dedicated to the baptism of Jesus. The years following 1967 witnessed several incidents in which PLO gunmen used explosives to demolish Christian churches. Priests were murdered in their shrines. It became obvious that these buildings, located just a dozen yards or so from the water's edge, were simply too vulnerable, and the entire Christian community was forced to evacuate.

The surviving churches were sealed and protected until a better time when they could be reopened for worship services. The Israelis strengthened their own position by fortifying the entire region with mines, barbed-wire entanglements, and other defenses.

With time, the PLO moved out of Jordan and shifted its base of operations to Lebanon. The strength of Israeli defenses, plus the removal of the PLO from Jordan, resulted in a meaningful reduction in the number of terrorists trying to infiltrate via the River Jordan. A *de facto* peace was created along the river, and in the early 1980s, farmers on both the Jordanian and Israeli sides of the river began planting crops in the fields behind their respective fortifications.

In 1982, the Greek Orthodox returned, for a few hours, to their Monastery of St. John the Baptist for a ceremony and worship service. Tensions were easing. Then, in 1985, the Roman Catholics returned to the shrine of *Qasr al-Yahud* — an Arab phrase that means "Jewish Fortress."

Israeli soldiers, responding to the eased tensions, removed the mines from the immediate vicinity of the Franciscan chapel.

Barbed wire was rolled back. Clearings were cut through the thickets, and open access was made right to the water's edge.

It was a joyous, although somewhat tense, occasion. Catholics have finally returned to the site of Jesus' baptism — but standing in this site, they stood between the loaded guns of two Middle Eastern armies technically in a state of war. And in the Middle East, the technicalities can be brushed aside for a murderous conflict without a moment's notice.

Had the Israelis contacted the Jordanian authorities to warn them that a Catholic procession would be wending its way to the Jordan River, a mere stone's throw from their front lines? Nobody is willing to say for sure, but it seems obvious that some sort of understanding must have been reached, because the Catholic service was conducted at the water's edge — literally twenty-five feet from Jordanian territory.

The fear and apprehension about wandering about in no-man's-land quickly pass. We are with hundreds of pilgrims and clergy. It is a sunny day, and the air is warm. There are constant prayers, chants, hymns, and incense. The tiny chapel is packed, so we remain outside and wander down to the water's edge. Here is the River Jordan, sacred river whose waters baptized Jesus. It must have been just as it is today. Both banks of the Jordan are shrouded with dense vegetation — a mixture of tall reeds, tropical bushes, and trees.

Four white egrets skim low over the river, flying about eighty yards upstream before alighting on the branches of a tamarisk tree that hangs out over the flow. A couple of dragonflies hover near us, unmindful of the many birds that would prey upon them. We reach down and touch the waters — cool and a bit murky, just as they should be. These waters start in the melting snows of Mount Hermon, only about 165 miles due north. In that distance, they tumble a vertical fall of about 10,500 feet — making this one of the steepest rivers on earth. Hermon is one of the highest peaks in the Middle East, at 9,232 feet. About three miles south of here, the Jordan flows into the Dead Sea which, at 1,312 feet below sea level, is the lowest point on earth.

Actually, most of the River Jordan is formed by several tributaries flowing from different parts of Mount Hermon — the Snir River, the Hermon River, the Dan River, and a few others. The Dan provides the greatest flow, hence the main river's name — Jordan — a contraction of the Hebrew *Yored Dan* which means "coming down from Dan."

We find a small stick and toss it into the water to time how long it takes to drift about a hundred yards downstream: about three and a half minutes. That calculates to just a bit slower than one mile an hour, not very fast at all. But the flow will quicken in a few months.when winter rains flood into the river.

It feels humid and tropical along the banks. There is a mixture of fragrances in the air. There are some animal tracks in the mud near the river's edge — they look like those of a swamp cat, a type of wildcat living in this region, about the size of an American bobcat or lynx.

For the most part, however, the banks of this meandering stream are rather steep; they don't permit much strolling by either man or beast.

It was in this region that St. John the Baptist preached the coming of the Messiah and baptized many people. According to the Gospel: "In the fifteenth year of the reign of Tiberius Caesar, Pontius Pilate being governor of Judea . . . the word of God came to John the son of Zechariah in the wilderness; and he went into all the region about the Jordan, preaching a baptism of repentance for the forgiveness of sins" (Lk 3:1-3).

Translating these dates from the Roman calendar, we can interpret the "fifteenth year of the reign of Tiberius Caesar" to be anytime during the year following August, A.D. 28.

Christian scholars generally agree that Jesus must have been between thirty-three and thirty-six years old at this time — which somewhat confounds calendar makers. Our modern calendars list years "A.D." — for *Anno Domini* (In the year of our Lord) — but according to scholars, Jesus could have been at least five years old at the beginning of the A.D. era.

The mistake appears to be linked to a misinterpretation of Luke 3:23 many centuries ago, when the calendar was brought into line with the Christian era. That passage of Scripture reads, "Jesus, when he started to teach, was about thirty years of age. . . ." That *"about"* means an imprecise age — although the calendar makers decided to construct a very precise calendar around it!

To reinforce this theory, it is well known that Jesus was born during the reign of Herod the Great. But historical records confirm time and again the Herod died in the year, 4 B.C. — which leaves us with the amusing paradox of Christ's appearing to have been born "Before Christ."

Such little inconsistencies infuriate some pedants, who spend so much effort fussing over details that they entirely miss the broader meanings. Jesus had little patience for such people, and challenged them: "You blind guides, straining out a gnat and swallowing a camel!" (Mt 23:24).

Baptism, incidentally, was a relatively common Jewish custom at the time of Jesus, and so the symbolic act of cleansing away sins was well understood by the many people who came to St. John. His most important baptism, certainly, was that of Jesus: "Then Jesus came from Galilee to the Jordan to John, to be baptized by him. John would have prevented him, saying, 'I need to be baptized by you, and do you come to me?' But Jesus answered him, 'Let it be so now, for thus it is fitting for us to fulfill all righteousness.' Then he consented. And when Jesus was baptized, he went up immediately from the water, and behold, the heavens were opened and he saw the Spirit of God descending like a dove and alighting on him; and lo, a voice from heaven saying, 'This is my beloved Son, with whom I am well pleased' " (Mt 3:13-17).

There is tremendous symbolism in the Spirit of God assuming the image of a dove, and this raises the gentle bird to a sacredly symbolic level of significance. Bible readers may recall that the dove is a symbol of renewed biological life: "The flowers appear on the earth, / the time of singing has come, / and the voice of the turtledove / is heard in our land" (Song 2:12). Here, the dove symbolizes a rejuvenated world growing in the warmth of spring, a new beginning for life.

With the story of the Flood, the dove becomes a more abstract symbol of life: ". . . and again he [Noah] sent forth the dove out of the ark; and the dove came back to him in the evening, and lo, in her mouth a freshly plucked olive leaf; so Noah knew that the waters had subsided from the earth" (Gen

8:10-11). This postdiluvian springtime was more symbolic than the annual passage of seasons because it was also the re-birth of a world purged of wickedness.

With the baptism of Jesus, the dove reaches its ultimate symbolic value and is identified with the Holy Spirit. The few drops of water that St. John sprinkled on Jesus may be viewed as the spiritual equivalent of the Flood. And this, again, was followed by the arrival of a dove proclaiming a new spring-time, proclaiming an end to an age of sin, proclaiming re-demption.

Thus, the dove became one of the most beautiful symbols of Scripture, a symbol of hope and goodness, a symbol of love. Is it any wonder, then, that when Jesus chased the merchants and money changers from the Temple in Jerusalem, He made a special effort to cast out the dove sellers?

The Franciscans and the Israeli authorities hope that this small portion of the River Jordan can be opened for pilgrims again, from time to time, for services and ceremonies to com-memorate the baptism of Jesus. And it's likely that this will be, for although the politicians in Israel and Jordan have not yet been able to negotiate a legal peace, there appears to exist a factual peace along the River Jordan.

The next stop on our pilgrimage brings us to Qumran, eight miles southwest of the baptismal site. Here, near the shores of the Dead Sea, we encounter the ruins of an ancient desert community. Not a tree, not a bush, not even a blade of grass grows in this harsh environment. It is oppressively hot — somewhere around one hundred twenty degrees in the shade — but the only shade to be found is under that little awning that covers the weather instruments. The air is parched dry. The desert all around is barren and strewn with jagged rocks and loose sand.

There is no record of Jesus ever having visited this site. No church or Christian shrine was ever built here. There is not even a single cross scratched into a lone rock. Nevertheless, the people who lived here had an incalculable influence on the growth and course of Christianity.

Qumran was built by the Essenes, a Jewish sect that broke away from mainstream Judaism about a century before the time of Jesus. They were purists — indeed, extremists — by the standards of ancient Israel, and also by the standards of today.

They came to this remote part of the desert so that they could be away from the rest of society and practice their faith with all the devotion and piety their laws required. Every detail of their personal lives was organized to provide love of God, constant goodness, and charity. Many of these details are known to us from the well-preserved records the Essenes kept — records which amount to one of the greatest archaeological discoveries of all time: the Dead Sea Scrolls.

There are about eight hundred scrolls that have been discovered in caves throughout this part of the desert, and they have all been linked to the Essenic sect at Qumran. Of these, about half have been opened and read during recent decades, and experts presume that the entire collection won't be totally revealed until at least the year 2000. The opening of each scroll is a difficult, time-consuming operation that requires the skill and patience of well-trained experts who have developed the best techniques for opening these twenty-century-old parchments.

The opened scrolls fall into two categories. One group includes the books of the Bible, and in them we have the oldest known copies of the Old Testament. Of vital importance today is the revelation that the texts of these ancient scrolls, and the texts of our modern Bibles, are identical. This confirms that, for example, when Jesus read from the Book of Isaiah in the synagogue of Capernaum (Capharnaum), His version contained the same text as modern versions. Anyone reading through recently published Hebrew texts of the Bible can match them word-by-word with the texts of the Dead Sea Scrolls.

The second group of scrolls includes philosophical statements of the Essenic community, as well as their internal laws, standards of conduct, and records of relations with others. The close correlation between this society and the early Christian community is astonishing. They shared many doctrines, and they had very similar liturgies. Their social organizations were also nearly a mirror image of each other's. There were, however, also several points of strong disagreement.

Many scholars think Jesus might have had substantial contact with the Essenes, and that early Christian development was very much influenced by this Jewish sect. The main issue which drove them apart was that of separatism. The Essenes wanted a closed community, where they could conduct their own affairs in their own way. They wanted as little contact as possible with the rest of the world. Christians, however, were obligated to "teach all nations" and bring the good news to anyone who would listen.

Climbing around the ruins of Qumran, we find that the Essenes organized a very communal lifestyle, with common dining halls and common storerooms.

Philo of Alexandria, a historian writing in A.D. 20, studied the Essenes and wrote that at that time they numbered about four thousand members. They were "worshipers of God, yet they did not sacrifice animals, regarding a reverent mind as the only true sacrifice." The Essenes, he wrote, avoided cities "to escape the contagion of evils. . . . They pursued agriculture and other peaceful arts; they accumulated neither gold nor silver, nor owned mines. No maker of warlike weapons, nor hucksters, nor traders by land or sea, was found among them. Least of all were any slaves found among them, for they saw in slavery a violation of the law of nature that made all men free brethren. . . . They taught piety, holiness, justice, the art of regulating home and city, knowledge of what is really good and bad and what is indifferent, what ends to avoid, what to pursue — in short, love of God, of virtue, and of man."

He added that the Essenes lived in colonies and welcomed visitors who were members of their sect. A community secretary received all earnings the members acquired, distributing clothing and articles that any members might need. Other ancient writers, including Eusebius, Josephus, and Pliny the

Elder, offered similar reports on this community of ascetics.

Their *Manual of Discipline* describes much of the sect's daily life: rising before sunup for prayer and work, at noontime they washed and dressed in white garments. The Essenes joined in the communal dining room for a sacramental midday meal. Afterward, they resumed their labors until evening, when they joined again for prayer and a meal.

The Essenes were strictly vegetarian; they declined all personal wealth; they practiced baptism; they maintained strict celibacy. Their numbers were kept strong by the constant recruitment of Jewish youngsters, and some scholars theorize that Jesus might have spent some time among the Essenes during His "hidden years" of adolescence.

As we tour the ruins of Qumran — the Essenic "capital" — we come to the remains of the *scriptorium*, a writing room where most, and perhaps all, of the Dead Sea Scrolls were drafted. Off to one side we find a large cistern, where the community kept its supplies of water — probably brought in with great effort from distant springs or perhaps even at the Jordan River before it emptied into the very salty Dead Sea. Here is a *mikvah*, a ceremonial bath where Essenes cleansed and purified themselves. Over there is the communal dining room. South of the community, across a small ravine, we can see a cave where the first scrolls were found. In the mountains to the west are many more caves, which yielded up a tremendous treasure of scrolls and knowledge of the ancient world.

Professor David Flusser, a highly respected scholar on early Christian communities, is "sure that Jesus knew the Essene positions, not only through John the Baptist, a dissident Essene, but that He met the Essenes themselves." Jesus knew the Essenes and criticized them, the scholar says. He notes that the Essenes called themselves the "sons of light" and that one of the most important of the Dead Sea Scrolls is entitled "The War of the Sons of Light with the Sons of Darkness," which relates a struggle between good and evil, with good eventually conquering at the End of Days.

It was the Essenic insistence on separating themselves

from the rest of the world that most annoyed Jesus. Professor Flusser cites the Gospel of St. Luke 16:1-12, the parable of the crafty steward, as being the statement of Jesus' essential disagreement with the Essenes. In this, Jesus uses a parable to create a Christian policy of using money, "tainted as it is," to secure friendship and good relations within their communities. Jesus encouraged His disciples to be worldly-wise, "for the sons of this world are wiser in their own generation than the sons of light" (16:8).

Knowing that the Essenes called themselves the "sons of light" and that they repudiated money and secular life makes this parable, and this particular passage, so much clearer.

Despite this schism, there are many other similarities that favorably link the Essenic and Christian communities, and a comparison of the Essenic *Manual of Discipline* and the Christian *Acts of the Apostles* offers many parallels in the organization of community life, beliefs, and policies.

Some scholars speculate that had it not been for the separation issue, and had the Essences been more inclined to go out into the world and practice their beliefs in open society, they would have formed one of the most important elements of early Christian society. Indeed, they suspect that the Christian worldly attitude might have drawn several Essenes away from the Qumran community to become leaders in the new Christian communities of Jerusalem and other cities. In the end, the worldliness of the Christian position brought that faith its great endurance and stature in humanity, while the reclusive monasticism of the Essenes resulted in their eventual disappearance.

The last Essenes died among the nine hundred sixty Jewish men, women, and children who defended themselves for a year against the Roman Tenth Legion at Masada. Excavations by the late Professor Yigal Yadin at the mountaintop fortress, located about thirty-five miles south of Qumran, revealed several Qumranic scrolls, thus confirming the claim by the historian Josephus that the Essenic "sons of light," who counted slavery as "a violation of the laws of nature," would not let themselves be taken prisoner to become Roman slaves. Rather, they accepted suicide — in their eyes, martyrdom — instead of living in a bondage that would prevent them from keeping their faith.

There is a craggy hill to the west of Qumran, and we climb up onto that rock to ponder the landscape below. The ruins of Qumran are spread right before us, and off to the left we can see where the Jordan River empties into the Dead Sea. A bit north of that is the baptismal site. These places are so close together that it seems impossible for them to exist in isolation. It seems without doubt that both Jesus and St. John the Baptist must have had some relationships with the Essenes. Yet the Gospels are almost silent. Except for that reference to the "sons of light," it would seem that there was no connection whatsoever between the Essenes and the early Christian community. Still, the first Christians had much more in common with the Essenes than they did with the scribes or the Pharisees, for example.

But perhaps it is because of this overall closeness that there is so little commonality. Who needs to preach to the converted? The vitality and the meaning of the Gospels can be found in the preachings of Jesus to people who differed with Him. Jesus did not have to tell the Essenes to "turn the other cheek," for this had been their doctrine for more than a century.

And, despite the very many similarities, the sole mention in the Gospels refers to the single outstanding distinction — the Essenic insistence upon removing themselves from contact with the outside world. But this only reinforces the basic thesis that much of the merit of the Gospels can be found in the contrasts between the teachings of Jesus and the accepted norms of society at that time. These are the preachings of reform, the good news that redirects human social behavior and human worship of God.

Many questions are left unanswered, and we are left to speculate. Sitting on this mountainside above the desert ruins, we think that perhaps Jesus did live among the Essenes right

The Holy Land

here at Qumran. It is possible that, as a child, He was sent here by Mary and Joseph to learn at something akin to an Essenic boarding school.

We know that the Essenes accepted youths into their ranks, and indeed this was the prime means of recruiting members. And we know that by the age of twelve Jesus was so well-versed in Scripture that He could astonish all the sages in the Temple of Jerusalem. Where did He learn so much? Probably not in Nazareth, which was a relatively poor town without any great centers of education. And probably not from His own Holy Family, for despite their wholesome goodness, they were but common townspeople, a carpenter and his wife.

Some people could say that Jesus didn't have to learn, He simply knew. But this would be denying Jesus part of His humanity. Jesus lived upon the earth as a man and encountered many human burdens. Some of these burdens were tremendous, most importantly the Passion and the temptation by the devil.

But also important were the many smaller burdens that Jesus shared with all humanity. As an infant, He had to be sheltered from the rages of the evil king Herod. He walked many miles across the Holy Land, suffering hunger and thirst. He suffered the prejudicial anti-Semitism of a Samaritan village, the contempt of the Pharisees, and bitter arguments with them. And one might also presume that He also had to endure the schoolboy's burdens of mastering His studies.

There are many mysteries concerning the "hidden years" of Jesus, and this offers us all sorts of possibilities for speculation. Modern scholars, however, are today solving many of those mysteries at an incredible rate, and to grasp some of this progress we must leave these desert ruins and drive about twenty miles westward, and about four thousand feet upward, to the mountaintop city of Jerusalem.

Here, in the Holy City, is the great repository of antiquity. Scores of museums house thousands, perhaps millions, of precious artifacts which reveal to us more and more about the everyday life of ancient Israel. In the Franciscan Museum, near the First Station of the Cross on the Via Dolorosa, there is a veritable treasure of artifacts from the time of Jesus. Detailed models show the various strata and discoveries of Catholic archaeological excavations beneath the Basilica of the Annunciation in Nazareth. There are simple, everyday utensils such as bowls and pots dating precisely from the time of Jesus, found in the ruins of communities He visited, such a Bethany, Cana, and of course, Jerusalem itself. There we can also view a pair of ancient fishing hooks positively dated to be about two thousand years old. They were discovered during the excavation of a building in Capharnaum, traditionally ascribed to be the home of St. Peter.

Other great collections also are to be found in Jerusalem, and any pilgrimage would be amiss if it did not tour a few of these. The Rockefeller Museum contains a great treasure of archaeological artifacts, and so does the Israel Museum, and many others. Of extreme importance is the Shrine of the Book, located on the grounds of the Israel Museum. Here, the Dead Sea Scrolls are kept in a special climate-controlled building. We wander through this unusual building and view biblical texts that were drafted at precisely the same time Jesus was preaching in this region.

Hundreds of scrolls remain unopened. We still have no idea what great revelations they contain. These scrolls are now being opened at the rate of about one a month, to be presented for the scrutiny of religious scholars, historians, and other experts. The process of opening a scroll — which has been tightly bound for twenty centuries and is so fragile that a single unprofessional mishap could destroy a priceless treasure — requires tremendous skill and patience. It is a process that reminds one of the most delicate and sophisticated of surgeries, which can be performed only by a very few of the world's most accomplished experts. And, fortunately for the scrolls, these experts are now on the staff of the Israel Museum's restoration laboratories.

While most of the scrolls are copies of biblical texts, or copies of the Essenic codes of behavior and religious philosophy, there are also found among them several miscellaneous writings — the community's financial accountings, records of supplies, and even letters. One important letter, for example, is correspondence between the Essenes and the hierarchy at the Temple of Jerusalem. Much of the substance of the letter involves the Essenic disagreement with Temple authorities — a complaint similar to that voiced by Jesus.

Christian scholars have strong hopes that somewhere among those as-yet-unopened scrolls there may be copies of correspondence between the Essenes and Christians.

Taken as a whole, all these artifacts illuminate the Gospels and increase our understanding of them. Because of the tremendous efforts in scholarship, archaeology, and other disciplines, we are today better able to understand the world where Christianity was born. We have a better grasp of the politics and struggles, everyday life and concerns — and we have better knowledge of those times than anyone since those times.

In A.D. 70, the Romans destroyed Jerusalem and many other communities of the Holy Land. Society was shattered, great institutions broken forever. A few decades after the Crucifixion, an entire society was horribly dispersed and its civilization buried under the rubble of conquest. Only today, in the twentieth century, is substantial progress being made at revealing that lost world by use of modern techniques of science and scholarship. And many of the key artifacts are to be seen carefully preserved in Jerusalem's many museums and shrines.

12 Lauda Sion... •
Jerusalem: Temple, Cenacle, Gethsemane

OUR SPECULATIONS about the early religious education of the young Jesus leads us to the great Temple of Jerusalem, for it was here that the twelve-year-old Child astonished the sages with His wisdom.

He astonished not just any sages, mind you, but the great doctors of the Temple. Understanding something about these scholars and the Temple is vital to understanding the religious climate that gave birth to Christianity — for it was the teachings of these scholars and the faith centered at this Temple that formed the most important root of Christian growth. Sometimes Jesus defended the words of the prophets, and sometimes He disputed the interpretations of His contemporaries. But for the most part, the teachings of Jesus are intimately linked to the practice of Judaism at His time.

The familiar Gospel story of the twelve-year-old Jesus in the Temple reveals much about this ancient institution. The Gospel makes an essential point in stressing that Jesus had separated himself from His family, causing them great anxiety, just so He could busy himself with His Father's affairs. He caused such concern because the sages and the Temple were unique. There were no equals — not at home in Nazareth, nor even in Athens or Rome or anywhere else in the world at that time.

Our pilgrimage today takes us to the remains of that Temple where Jesus first revealed His greatness, and where later he would return on several occasions to debate the scribes and Pharisees. It is possible to stand in the Temple's shadow and to touch its ancient stones. This is the Western Wall — one of the most important religious shrines in the world. When one understands the significance of the Wall, and of the Temple of which it was part, one can also understand why the youthful Jesus was impelled to leave His family so He could discuss religious affairs with the great scholars who sat there.

The Temple was first built by the mighty King Solomon during the years around 960 B.C. The First Book of Kings describes the great building, a magnificent structure where cascades of fresh flowers were heaped upon altars of gold, and where in the springtime the wise son of David gathered the nation to dedicate the Temple of God.

The Temple was built upon a great rock known as Moriah (pronounced Mo-*ree*-ah in Hebrew), the rock upon which Abraham offered the life of his son Isaac to the command of God. Once the Temple was built, Solomon moved the Ark of the Covenant, the first tabernacle, built by Moses three centuries before, to the most sacred chambers of the Temple — the Holy of Holies. In subsequent centuries, the Temple became the center of Jewish religious, communal, and scholarly life.

It is even safe to say that the Temple became the very center of Judaism — for here most of the great prophets and saints of Scripture imparted their wisdom, their prophetic gifts, and their holiness.

When Nebuchadnezzar conquered Jerusalem during 587 B.C., he carried the Jews away to bondage in Babylon. And from that bondage comes a most ancient prayer, which reveals the exiles' yearnings to return home to the City of the Temple: "By the waters of Babylon, there we sat down and wept, / when we remembered Zion. . . . / If I forget you, O Jerusalem, / let my right hand wither! / Let my tongue cleave to the roof of my mouth, / if I do not remember you, / if I do not set Jerusalem above my highest joy!" (Ps 137 [136]:1, 5-6).

Seventy years later, when King Cyrus of Persia won control of the Babylonian Empire, he freed the Jews and they returned to Jerusalem to rebuild their Temple, the Temple of Zerubbabel, dedicated in 515 B.C.. The great joy of the restoration is related in the gifted writings of Isaiah, Ezra, and Nehemiah. And the Second Temple reassumed the prominence of its predecessor, gathering to it all the greatest religious and intellectual vitality of the nation.

By the time Jesus entered the Temple, the institution had a history of nearly a thousand years. It was a structure that inspired, a structure that aroused the strongest sentiments of the Jewish people. It was a building dedicated to the First Commandment of God: "I am the LORD your God. . . . You shall have no other gods before me" (Ex 20:2-3).

History reveals the single-minded devotion the Jews had to this Commandment and to the Temple, which was the most important structure honoring God. For example, when Alexander the Great marched through Israel, the Jews acquiesced to the stronger Greek rule. But when Antiochus, a successor of Alexander, imposed Greek pagan worship in the Temple, the Jews rose in fanatical revolt against a much stronger army — and drove them out of the Temple, purified the building, and rededicated it to God. This rededication is commemorated each year in the Jewish festival of Hannukah.

All this had passed by the time the young Jesus entered the sacred precincts. Herod the Great had begun a new Temple in 19 B.C. At that time there were two groups of Jewish sages associated with the Temple. The Pharisees were strong advocates of religious influence over daily life. They were members of a sect that made great efforts to discourage Jews from adopting foreign modes, expecially the casual cultures of Greece and Rome. They were the religiously orthodox who grew up after the return from Babylonian captivity. The Pharisees were generally ascetic, with little regard for wealth or pleasures. By the time of Jesus, however, there were several complaints that they had grown too formal, that they had become pedantic in their interpretations of religious law, that they had begun to lose sight of the human elements of religion.

The Sadducees were the Temple aristocracy. They focused their attention on Jewish law as written in the first five books of the Bible. Unlike the Pharisees, they tended to ignore their traditions and were not inclined to interpret and debate various merits. Some scholars presume that the Sadducees organized to counterbalance the influence of the Pharisees and to offer greater emphasis to the Law of Moses. The Sadducees were more tolerant of foreign influence as long as it did not interfere with the exercise of Jewish law.

The Gospels do not tell us which group the young Jesus spoke with — perhaps both — but it is apparent that this may have been the beginning of His lifelong disputing with the Pharisees. In later years, Jesus often challenged the Pharisees because of their devotion to pedantry: "Woe to you, scribes and Pharisees, hypocrites! For you tithe mint and dill and cummin, and have neglected the weightier matters of the law, justice and mercy and faith; these you ought to have done, without neglecting the others. You blind guides, straining out a gnat and swallowiong a camel!" (Mt 23:23-24).

Much of the essence of Christian thought was to develop from the debates Jesus had with the Pharisees of the Temple. Sometimes these debates were quite heated, and Gospels record that even the moderate Jesus was inclined to use harsh words when addressing the Pharisees, and at various times He called them "blind guides" (Mt 15:14), "serpents, you brood of vipers" (23:33), and other epithets which probably provoked their anger. But the use of such harsh language reveals something of the character of the Temple at the time of Jesus. Indeed, the simple fact that a boy of twelve years could stand in the midst of the sages is also revealing.

The Temple was a lively institution. In addition to being a building of worship, it also had a long history of serving as an intellectual, philosophical, and religious forum where various sects challenged one another with speeches and debates. The Temple was the vibrant seat of Judaic culture. At times, some people took advantage of the liberal policies of the Temple and abused them by introducing commerce and other non-spiritual activities into the Temple precincts. Christians are familiar with Jesus chasing the dove sellers and money changers from the Temple, but they should also know that Jesus was not the first reformer of this sort. Periodically through the preceding thousand years, reformers had forcibly challenged abusers of the Temple's sacred functions, and often with great success.

Despite the occasional abuse, the Temple served the nation admirably for a millennium. The greatness crumbled shortly after the time of Jesus. In A.D. 70, the Temple was destroyed, and paganism again figured in the struggle. A few years earlier, the Emperor Nero had tried to impose the worship of his Roman pantheon on the Jews and brought desecration to the Temple. Predictably, the Jews rebelled. But this time the might of the foreign invader was simply too great for even the most spirited resistance. As revenge against the revolt, Rome destroyed Jerusalem and its Temple. About one million Jews were killed in the fighting, and the survivors were exiled. The Roman conquerors issued an edict which prohibited Jews from approaching the ruins of Jerusalem under penalty of death.

Yet a remnant remained. A few Jews stayed behind in Judea and the Land of Israel to maintain ancient traditions. And a part of the great Temple still stood — its Western Wall.

Through the next twenty centuries, Jews had no sovereignty in their ancient homeland. Their fortunes ebbed and flowed with the policies of whoever occupied the land — after the Romans came the Byzantines and the Persians, then the Arabs and Seljuks, the Crusaders and the Mamluks, the Ottoman Turks and the British. In 1948, when the British abandoned their mandate, Israel's War of Independence found Jerusalem — for the first time in its very ancient history — split in two. And the Western Wall fell to the Arab side. Through the next nineteen years, despite guarantees in the cease-fire agreements, Jews were prohibited from approaching the Western Wall, and it was not until the Six-Day War of 1967 that Israeli paratroopers wrested the Western Wall and the Temple precincts from the hands of the Arab Legion.

Today, it is possible for the casual tourist of any faith to approach the Western Wall. A broad plaza has been cleared before it, and various facilities have been installed to provide for the comfort and security of pilgrims. In many ways, the Western Wall has reassumed the heritage of the Temple. On any day it is possible to find preachers making speeches to any-one who will listen. Many Israelis consecrate their marriages at the Wall. Bar Mitzvahs — the Jewish parallel for Confirmation — are conducted here. It is a place for private prayer and spirituality. There are many traditions associated with it, and one of the most appealing is that of writing messages to God on a piece of paper, folding it and stuffing it in any of the cracks between the great stones in the Wall. There must be millions of such papers crammed there. On holidays, particularly festive ones such as *Simhath Torah* (Joy of the Law), the plaza before the Wall is filled with people singing, praying, dancing, and proclaiming eternal devotion to God and His Commandments.

In orthodox Jewish tradition, this Wall is the closest an observant Jew should approach the Temple precincts. Going above the wall, to where the Dome of the Rock now stands, is forbidden — for much the same reason that observant Catholics would not intrude into a tabernacle in their churches.

Recent studies of the Temple Mount region have opened much controversy, as some Jews want to remove the Dome of the Rock — a Muslim shrine — and replace it with a new Temple. This has caused much strife, although it is the work of but a small minority. Similarly, there are Christians who want to reconvert the Al Aksa mosque — which also stands on Temple Mount — to use as a church.

Al Aksa (or El Aqsa) was originally built as the Church of the Virgin during the Byzantine rule, but with the Islamic conquests of A.D. 629 it was converted into a mosque, and it remains in that use to this day. Christian shrines around Jerusalem are so numerous that it would be impossible to describe them all in a single chapter — or a single book, for that matter. It is important, however, for us to visit the most significant shrines, and also to gain a feeling for this great city in the mountains.

To gain a broad perspective of Jerusalem, we hike down to the southern wall, near the Dung Gate, whence we can walk along the ancient parapets of the city. Recently restored, this

"Rampart Walk" follows the walls of the Old City and offers a series of panoramic vistas in all directions. To our east, we can see the Mount of Olives standing close by the city. It is still planted with many olive groves, and between it and Jerusalem yawns the chasms of Kidron Valley, to which we shall return later.

Walking along the south wall we see the Arab village of Silwan nestled against the hills. Right at our feet, flush against the rampart wall, is a new archaeological park, which reveals excavations dating back to the time of King Solomon. It is open to the general public and is known as the Biblical Archaeology Park.

In these remains, archaeologists uncovered a broad flight of steps leading up to Temple Mount. They hadn't seen the light of day since that terrible hour in the year 70 when Roman soldiers destroyed the Temple and tossed its stones down over the wall, burying these stairs in the debris. Newly excavated, they assure that pilgrims can now walk upon the same steps where certainly Jesus walked, and all the apostles and disciples, too.

There are many other impressive sites in this park, some as ancient as the ritual baths — or *mikvahs* — used nine centuries before Jesus. Archaeologists have also identified and partially restored finely crafted homes from the Christian Byzantine period, and mosaic floors from the Muslim Omayyad era. The remains of the Byzantine Nea Church are, in part, incorporated into the structure of the present wall.

Inside the old walls we see the new Jewish Quarter. In 1948, when the Arab Legion took control of this area, they demolished the old Jewish Quarter along with several dozen synagogues — some dating back for many centuries. When the Israelis regained control in 1967, they launched a major renovation and reconstruction effort, which restored and maintained much of the old Jerusalem architecture.

Following the wall, we pass the Armenian Quarter on the inside, and Mount Zion on the outside. Mount Zion is intimately attached to the rich history of Jerusalem. Indeed, in many places of the Bible, when a prophet writes of "Zion," he means Jerusalem itself. The crest of this hill is only a few acres in area, but contains an extremely important variety of religious sites which must be visited.

It is here, on the forested slopes of Mount Zion, that we can visit the ancient Tomb of King David. We enter the building, cross about forty feet of the main hall, and enter a smaller prayer room. It is cool and shadowy. Through a barred door, against the east wall, we can see the velvet-draped tomb — a great block of limestone which seals the remains of Jesus' noble ancestor in the earth below.

We offer a prayer, and our respects, to the memory of this great man. It was for him that Bethlehem was known as the "City of David," and because Joseph was of the line of David, he had to return to David's birthplace for the Roman census — and for this, Jesus was born in Bethlehem. King David made Jerusalem his capital, and initiated the custom of focusing the practice of Judaism in Jerusalem.

We leave the prayer room, walk across the hall, and climb a flight of stone steps to a second story — the Cenacle, the *Coenaculum*, the Hall of the Last Supper.

This is the "upper room" of the Gospels: ". . . on the first day of Unleavened Bread, when they sacrificed the passover lamb, his [Jesus'] disciples said to him, 'Where will you have us go and prepare for you to eat the Passover?' And he sent two of his disciples, and said to them, 'Go into the city, and a man carrying a jar of water will meet you; follow him, and wherever he enters, say to the householder, "The Teacher says, Where is my guest room, where I am to eat the passover with my disciples?" And he will show you a large *upper room* [italics mine] furnished and ready; there prepare for us" (Mk 14:12-15).

The Cenacle (from the Latin *cena*, "supper") actually has three rooms on the upper story — one large room and two smaller ones. The large room measures about fifty by forty feet, with a stone floor and two exquisite pillars supporting a vaulted ceiling. The architecture is decidedly medieval, and there is little likelihood that the Last Supper could have actually taken place in this particular room. However, according to Christian tradition, this more recent "large upper room" marks the precise site where the original "large upper room" existed. Tradition holds that the original room was destroyed during the catastrophic Roman sacking of Jerusalem in A.D. 70.

No other traditions contradict the Cenacle as being the site of the Last Supper, and it is reasonable to assume that this was the site of the institution of the Eucharist.

The Gospels tell us that Jesus came here to celebrate Passover, and the traditional method of celebrating this feast is with a ritual meal and the reading of the Haggadah — a narrative liturgy that recalls the Exodus of the Children of Israel from Egyptian slavery. And in this liturgy, which is the oldest continuously practiced religious ceremony of humanity, we find many of the roots of our modern Mass. Passover commemorates a physical redemption, a deliverance from slavery — and the Eucharist is a spiritual redemption and a deliverance from a spiritual slavery. The Passover meal contains many elements. In addition to the unleavened bread (matzo) and wine, there are also roasted lamb, hard-boiled eggs, bitter herbs, sweets, and other dishes — each representing symbolically an element of the Exodus.

Jesus took two of the most important symbols — the matzo and wine — and vastly expanded their significance: ". . . when the hour came, he sat at table, and the apostles with him. And he said to them, 'I have earnestly desired to eat this passover with you before I suffer; for I tell you I shall not eat it until it is fulfilled in the kingdom of God.' And he took a cup, and when he had given thanks he said, 'Take this, and divide it among yourselves; for I tell you that from now on I shall not drink of the fruit of the vine until the kingdom of God comes.' And he took bread, and when he had given thanks he broke it and gave it to them, saying, 'This is my body which is given for you. Do this in remembrance of me.' And likewise the cup after supper, saying, 'This cup which is poured out for

The Holy Land

you is the new covenant in my blood' " (Lk 22:14-20; cf Mt, Mk).

And it was done here, in a room that existed at this site, so very long ago. At the far right corner of the room there are a few steps that lead up through a portal into a second, smaller room, and from here there is a passage to a third small room, and in this third room there is a cenotaph, or memorial, to King David, who lies directly beneath.

One important question often comes to pilgrims visiting this room of the Last Supper: Although the Last Supper is mentioned in all four Gospels, not one of them also mentions that it was conducted in a room directly above the tomb of David. Why was this not mentioned?

The surest answer is that the fact was known to Jesus alone, and He chose not to tell anyone at that time.

King David died nearly a thousand years before the Last Supper, and this shepherd-king's tomb had been a well-known site outside the Jerusalem city walls for centuries until 587 B.C., when Nebuchadnezzar conquered and destroyed the city. David's tomb was buried in the rubble.

A generation later, when the Jews returned to Jerusalem, many of the ancient sites were lost, unknown. Through later centuries, the city expanded. Mount Zion was included within newer walls, and new buildings, including the Cenacle, were built upon the ancient rubble. At the time of the Last Supper, nobody except Jesus himself knew that this vitally important ritual was being initiated immediately above the last resting place of His royal ancestor.

It was not until A.D. 1158 that David's tomb was discovered. In that year, the Crusaders were repairing the Cenacle and found beneath it the remains of an older structure, which they thought to demolish, using the stones for their own construction work. But upon probing the region, they found that the stone sealed an underground tomb, which proved, upon closer examination, to be that of King David.

Four hundred years later, the Ottoman Turks rebuilt the walls of Jerusalem, and along this southern flank they built the wall in a new location which left Mount Zion outside the city again, and so it remains today, with the tomb beyond the wall.

Another important shrine nearby is Dormition Abbey, a Benedictine monastery commemorating the "Sleep of Saint Mary" (*Dormitio Sanctae Mariae*). It is here, according to tradition, that our Lady passed into eternal sleep.

The Church is one of the most popular in Jerusalem because of its beauty and its music; here biweekly organ concerts have attracted music-lovers of all faiths. There's a crypt beneath, and here we see a statue of our Lady upon her deathbed with Jesus calling His mother to heaven. An inscription from the Bible reads: ". . . Arise, my love, my fair one, and come away" (Song 2:13).

Our Lady was carried from here to a crypt in the Valley of Kidron, northeast of here, and laid to rest. From there she was taken to heaven, body and soul, at the Assumption.

Surrounding the crypt are medallions of important women of the Old Testament — Eve, Miriam, Jael (*Ya'el*), Judith, Ruth, and Esther.

Outside, and not far away, is another crypt, the *Martef Ha'Shoah*, the Chamber of the Martyrs, a memorial to the six million Jews who were murdered by the Nazis during the Holocaust for the simple reason that they were Jewish.

The hillside rolls away into a deep valley — *Gei Hinnom*, the Valley of Hinnom. This is Gehenna, the valley of the damned.

It is a somber vale, part grassland, part olive orchard, and part outcroppings of bedrock. In remote antiquity, pagans sacrificed children here by throwing them into the fires of the Canaanite god Moloch. Here, in this sad abyss, stood Tophet, the place of punishment for the wicked. This is the place of hell. And it was here that Judas Iscariot ran, after betraying Jesus, and hanged himself.

Our tour upon Jerusalem's walls leads us now northward to Jaffa Gate and the ancient citadel — the main fortress of the city, rebuilt many times over. We can discern the additions made by the Ottomans, the Crusaders, and the Byzantines. But there is still much of the Roman-period edifice still standing — ramparts which protected this part of the city since before the time of Jesus.

Onward still, upon the walls of Jerusalem, we pass by the Latin Patriarchate, the official residence of the Roman Catholic (Latin) Patriarch of Jerusalem, the spiritual leader of the Holy Land's Catholic community. Just beyond this is the Frères School, one of Jerusalem's several parochial schools. We turn the northwest corner and soon pass Saint Savior, the Franciscan church and monastery, seat of the Custos — the custodian of all Catholic shrines in the Holy Land.

Throughout this entire area within the city walls is the Christian Quarter of Jerusalem. Scores, perhaps hundreds, of shrines, chapels, grottos, and churches exist here, each with its own special meaning and rich history, each a distinct testament to Christian devotion to Jerusalem. There are many streets and alleys, which wander back and forth through the quarter with its venerable stone buildings and tiny shops — an interesting neighborhood to wander.

But we haven't the time to tarry right now. Onward we follow the old wall, past the "New Gate," and eastward to the battlements above "Damascus Gate." From here, there is a magnificent vista of the city. Outside the walls, Arab East Jerusalem spreads before us, and up the hill to our left, in Jewish West Jerusalem, we can see the imposing Notre Dame de France, a century-old monastery recently acquired by the Vatican from the Pères Augustins de l'Assomption and converted into one of the finest pilgrims' hostels in the city.

On the inside of the city wall, the many domes and spires of Jerusalem spread before us, and there is an engraved bronze plate here that helps us identify the most important landmarks. Peering down from the wall, we see one of the busiest streets of Jerusalem — El-Wad, which branches off, just a few yards southward, to Khan ez-Zeit. These are "pedestrian-only" streets, for there is no room for a motor vehicle. Pedestrians, however, may also include a few of the four-legged variety, as well as an occasional pushcart. Within a few minutes we see Arab women, with trays of fresh-baked sesame breads balanced precariously on their heads; a group of orthodox Jews, hurrying off in the direction of the Western Wall; two Franciscan friars, in their brown robes and sandals, strolling toward the Christian Quarter; a young boy leading a reluctant donkey, loaded with burlap-wrapped packages; and hundreds of other people from an incredible diversity of cultural and religious backgrounds.

A quick visit to the foot of Damascus Gate leads us to more archaeological excavations. Here we can view the newly discovered Roman gate to the city and, through it, enter a gallery with a small but appealing archaeological museum.

Farther east, we follow Sultan Suleiman Street, past Solomon's stone quarry and the pretty Flower Gate to the northeast corner of the city. Here, we turn right and follow Jericho Road for about five hundred yards into Kidron Valley.

Here, just east of the old city walls of Jerusalem, we stand amid many extremely important Christian shrines. Fifteen minutes' walk to the southwest brings us to St. Peter-in-Gallicantu Church, which commemorates St. Peter's triple denial of Jesus (see Lk 22:54-62) and his repentance after hearing the crowing of the cock (thus the name *gallicantu*). Just north of this lovely church archaeologists have unearthed an ancient stairway which leads from the traditional site of the Last Supper — the Cenacle — to Gethsemane, and thus was very likely the path which Jesus walked mere hours before His arrest. Scientific studies of the stairs positively identify that they were in use at the time of Jesus and subsequently buried in A.D. 70 when the Romans razed the Temple and much of Jerusalem.

Eastward we walk from St. Peter's, through thorny brush, past the bottom of the stairs, up and down small hills, and by a number of archaeological sites. Here is a tunnel built at the time of King Hezekiah to carry water into Jerusalem. There are the remains of the Jebusite wall and the city King David captured three thousand years ago. And over there is Haceldama, or Akeldama — the Field of Blood, which was purchased with the thirty pieces of silver paid to Judas for betraying Jesus. After Judas's suicide, the money was used to buy a cemetery for strangers who died in Jerusalem (see Mt 27:3-10). Here also, Greek Orthodox monks tend the Monastery of St. Oniprius, and they show pilgrims a cave, hewn from the bedrock, where centuries of tradition claim that the apostles hid during the trial of Jesus.

A bit northward we pass through the Valley of Jehoshaphat, an alternate name for this part of the Kidron Valley. And here we see great ancient tombs — the cone-peaked Absalom's Pillar, traditional burial site of Absalom, the son of King David. Then there are Jehoshaphat's Tomb and the Grotto of St. James, traditional resting spot of the cousin of Jesus. Jews and Christians differ as to who was buried in the Tomb of Zechariah — the Old Testament prophet or the husband of Elizabeth and father of St. John the Baptist?

Farther up the valley, we pass the Church of St. Stephen, a Greek Orthodox shrine built on the traditional site of the first Christian martyrdom. Across the road is the Church of the Assumption, and Christian historians say that once our Lady died on Mount Zion, she was carried here to rest, and from here she was assumed into heaven. Inside this crypt one may also find the tombs of several pious Crusader women who died in Jerusalem during the period of the Latin Crusader Kingdom.

A narrow passageway from the courtyard leads us to the Grotto of Gethsemane. This is the natural cavern where Jesus often met with His disciples, and here we take a moment from our hectic pace to sit and read: ". . . he came out, and went, as was his custom, to the Mount of Olives; and the disciples followed him. And when he came to the place he said to them, 'Pray that you may not enter into temptation.' And he withdrew from them about a stone's throw, and knelt down and prayed, 'Father, if thou art willing, remove this cup from me; nevertheless not my will, but thine, be done.' And there appeared to him an angel from heaven, strengthening him. And being in an agony he prayed more earnestly, and his sweat became like great drops of blood falling down upon the ground. And when he rose from prayer, he came to the disciples and found them sleeping for sorrow, and he said to them, 'Why do you sleep? Rise and pray that you may not enter into temptation' " (Lk 22:39-46).

Above this grotto and a few yards south is the perfectly tended Garden of Gethsemane. It is a tranquil garden with many flowers growing at every time of year. Within this garden, we find eight gnarled olive trees, each at least a thousand years old. According to Christian tradition, these trees grew from shoots that were clipped from the trees that grew here at the time of Jesus' agony.

Gethsemane, incidentally, takes its name from the Hebrew *gat shemen* — a *gat* is a stone press, and *shemen* means "oil." Through much of antiquity, olives which grew upon the Mount of Olives were collected in this area and crushed for their oil.

On the southern edge of this lovely garden is the magnificent Basilica of the Agony, which is also known as the Church of All Nations because of the many communities from around the world that helped to fund its construction. Dedicated by the Franciscans in 1924, this truly marvelous church stands upon the ruins of several others, including major basilicas dating from the Crusader and Byzantine periods.

Richly decorated, the basilica is a treasure of Christian art. A fine mosaic stretches across the full width of the entrance, depicting Jesus and His disciples praying during those last hours in Gethsemane. Within the basilica there's a soft and unusual light that filters in through the church's translucent alabaster windows. The roof is made from twelve matching domes, the ceiling side of which are decorated with a number of artworks unique to the many countries that contributed to the church's construction.

The altar is set at the eastern end of the basilica, upon a massive protrusion of bedrock — the Rock of the Agony. It was here that Jesus met with His disciples and roused them from their sleepiness. It was here that He was arrested:

"While he was still speaking, Judas came, one of the twelve, and with him a great crowd with swords and clubs, from the chief priests and the elders of the people. Now the betrayer had given them a sign, saying, 'The one I shall kiss is the man; seize him.' And he came up to Jesus at once and said, 'Hail, Master!' And he kissed him" (Mt 26:47-49).

From here, Jesus was led away to trial, and the disciples fled in fear.

Each year, as part of the Passion pageantry in Jerusalem, very moving ceremonies are conducted in Gethsemane. And at any time of year, one may come to visit the grotto, the gardens, and the basilica to ponder the tragic events that started from this place.

We sit beneath one of the ancient olive trees in the quiet of the garden and think of the quality of prayer. Catholics will recall that Jesus taught the disciples the Our Father when they said to Him, "Lord, teach us to pray. . ." (see Lk 11:1-4). But here, we understand that this is only part of prayer — knowing the holy and tremendously meaningful words. But *how* to pray includes more than mere words. It includes an intensity of devotion and attention. We see it in the Gospels, which tell us that when Jesus prayed, "his sweat became like great drops of blood falling down upon the ground" (Lk 22:44).

Is it possible for any of us to pray with such fervor?

13

Via Dolorosa •
The Street of Sorrows
to the Crucifixion

IT IS A WARM spring morning. The sky is clear blue, and the air is fragrant with the many sweet smells of Jerusalem. We meet at St. Stephen's Gate, on the eastern side of the Old City's walls. According to tradition, the first Christian martyr died near here, and his sacrifice is recalled by the mere mention of this portal to the Holy City.

A narrow cobblestone streets leads into the city, and in a minute we pass by the iron gate to St. Anne's Church. Within is a lovely garden, an excavated archaeology site, and an imposing church. The church is built on the site of the home of Sts. Anne and Joachim, and it was here that their daughter, Mary, was born.

The archaeological excavations outside the church include the remains of a Crusader church and the ancient Pools of Bethesda, where Jesus came to heal the sick. A small but very interesting archaeology museum is also located at this site.

There is an inclination to step in and visit this lovely sanctuary, for it embraces so much happiness — the site of the Blessed Virgin's birth, the site of miraculous healing by the hand of Jesus: such goodness happened here. But we put this visit off for another day. On today's pilgrimage, we follow the route of suffering and death. We should not seek to soften the intensity of sadness along the Via Dolorosa.

A few yards farther on into the city, along this same street, we come to a small, recently built plaza where several groups of pilgrims are gathered, and here we meet with Yitzhak Yaacovy, an Israeli Jew who for more than a decade took charge of renovations all along the Via Dolorosa. "When we studied the renovation plans of the Via Dolorosa," Yaacovy says, "we realized that there was no meeting place where pilgrims could gather before beginning the Stations of the Cross. So we built this plaza." He explains that today, of all the shrines in Christendom, the Via Dolorosa probably has the most profound meaning. And in order for pilgrims to get a deeper appreciation of this Street of Sorrows, it is useful for them to have a place like this to gather, to talk with their guide or priest, and perhaps to offer a prayer or two before walking the length of this terrible way.

"In the depth of their feelings, most pilgrims don't realize what we have done here," Yaacovy notes. "In fact, few people anywhere take much notice of what isn't seen." But here, and all along the Via Dolorosa, the most important improvements are the ones nobody sees.

Until the Israeli-funded renovations, sewage ran through the storm drains along the Via Dolorosa. The stench kept many pilgrims away. Electric and telephone wires cluttered up the sky. In several places, the street simply collapsed as centuries-old underground ducts crumbled under the weight above them. The Via Dolorosa was constantly defaced with garbage and trash, and along nearly its entire length there was no public lighting.

"We made a total renovation," Yaacovy says. "We put new sewage pipes into the ground, and at the same time we installed underground conduit pipes for electricity, telephone, and even cable television. We cleaned up the entire area, put in new street lamps and direction signs in several languages, and then we repaved the entire Via Dolorosa."

The repaving itself is a most tasteful and meaningful job. Along most of the Way of the Cross, simple cobblestones are laid upon the street in regular, staggered lines. At each Station, however, a simple Roman number on the nearest wall marks the site, and the paving stones there are laid in concentric circles radiating outward. Some parts of the Via Dolorosa are paved with massive, ancient pavement stones dating from the days of Rome. These great stones, which measure about two by three feet, were unearthed by Israeli archaeologists as they excavated among the ruins of Roman Jerusalem. But rather than set them in a museum, they had them restored to their original use, and now the stones are walked upon by the many thousands of pilgrims who come each year to follow the Way of the Cross. How many Roman chariots thundered across these stones? Was this piece trod upon by the early Christians? Or by the apostles? Or even Jesus himself? If only they could tell us their true histories!

We look around the little plaza at the beginning of the Via Dolorosa and see that it is both functional and esthetic. A map of the Via Dolorosa, inscribed in a large bronze plaque, shows the route before us. A granite stone, dedicated by the Cathedral of St. John the Divine in New York City, is set in a place of honor within the plaza's southern retaining wall. There are benches made of cut limestone from the Judean mountains, and a garden of biblical plants — persimmon, myrtle, and olive — garlands the site.

"I love the little details and the dimensions of the inner story. These are dimensions of meaning rather than size," Yaacovy says. "We concentrated a lot of attention to detail here, and this is the only way to make restoration in Jerusalem, because evey site, every stone, has within it a tremendous history. There is so much profundity all around us.

"Perhaps in giant cities like New York or London or Paris, architects can work on grand scales, but it is not possible here," he says. "There is no cathedral in the world that arouses greater sentiment and religious feeling for Christians than the simple, open street of the Via Dolorosa.

1 never heard of the Via Dolorosa before coming to Israel," Yaacovy admits. "But now, I know quite a bit about it." Not only does this chief restorer know the physical dimensions of the ancient street, but he also knows all the historical references, including a verbatim memory of the Gospels.

"I love Jerusalem," he proclaims, "and therefore I love my job, because my job is the restoration of this greatest city. I thrive on the responsibility. I gather the best talent I can find and focus on detail, detail, and more detail. We work together, and we are proving something. We are proving that Israel is

The Holy Land

responsible and takes good care of the holy places here. We are making vital restorations that were ignored by the Jordanians, and by the British before them, and by the Turks before them.''

Yaacovy continues to talk about his many concerns along the Via Dolorosa, and especially about the desire to maintain it as a "living street" — with people and donkeys and carts moving up and down conducting the business of life — just as it was two thousand years ago. The Passion of Jesus was not experienced in solitude, he reminds us. The sad street leading from the Antonia Fortress to Calvary was a busy thorough-fare, teeming with merchants, beggars, shoppers, and soldiers. And to get some of the "feeling" of the Via Dolorosa, it's important that the pilgrim following the Way of the Cross rub shoulders with the Jerusalemites who daily crowd upon this sacred street.

Yaacovy's intensity and great concern for precision was born in a most tragic past. The man who restored the Street of Sorrow has known tremendous sorrow himself.

He was born between the World Wars in a religious Jew-ish family in Hungary. With the start of World War II, the young schoolboy was herded into the enclosed Jewish Quarter of Debrecen with his family, relatives, and other Jews. As the war intensified, the ghetto was closed down and its Jews moved to various concentration camps. In 1944, they were all moved to Auschwitz and fed into the mass-execution machine, with its gas chambers and ovens. The Nazis worked around the clock to murder all the Jews, and through one forty-six-day period their records indicate that at least a quarter-million Jews were executed and fed into the crematoria. That number included all of Yaacovy's family.

In spite of their great energy, the Nazis simply couldn't kill the vast numbers of people they had imprisoned, and when the Soviet Red Army approached Auschwitz in January of 1945, the surviving Jews were force-marched through the win-ter snows in a retreat to Austria, where young Yitzhak Ya acovy escaped. He hid for four months, fearing recapture and execution simply because he was a Jew. In May of 1945, he found liberation at the hands of the U.S. Third Army.

Yitzhak was then tended in a hospital where he and many other surviving children had to be tied to their beds. Some who broke away raided the kitchens and were killed by what amounted to a simple meal. Their emaciated bodies could not stand so many nutrients at one time. Recovery had to be gradual. As he recovered, Yitzhak made contact with a few members of the British Army's Jewish Brigade. With Hitler crushed, these Palestinian Jews were interested in returning home and bringing with them the remnant of Jews who survived the Holocaust. In 1947, he boarded an "illegal immigrant" freighter — the S.S. *Moda'i Haghettaot* — on a course to the shores of Palestine. The ship was intercepted by the British Royal Navy near Haifa, and its passengers were escorted to a prison camp on Cyprus.

Yitzhak was trained as a soldier by undercover instructors of the Haganah, the informal Jewish army of Palestine, while he was in the British camp. Within months, the British had abandoned Palestine and five Arab armies had attacked the infant State of Israel. There were only some three thousand trained professional soldiers in the Israeli ranks when the war broke out, and these were reinforced by about fifty thousand part-time volunteer shopkeepers, farmers, housewives, and even schoolchildren. A Reuters dispatch from Cairo estimated the strength of the Egyptian Army alone to be about two hundred thousand men equipped with tanks and artillery.

Yitzhak Yaacovy was one of the young men rushed into Israel as soon as the British had left Palestine and disbanded their prison camps on Cyprus. After a quick orientation in his new home and new army, he was thrown into battle as part of the Giv'ati Brigade, which dug in their defenses around Kibbutz Negba, about twenty-five miles south of Tel Aviv. The battle was furious — one of the most intense of the entire war — but the vastly outnumbered Jewish defenders stopped the entire Egyptian Army. Counterattacks sent the Egyptians into a disorganized retreat. They kept falling back until they were out of the territory that the United Nations had allocated to the new State of Israel. When the smoke of battle had cleared, medical corpsmen lifted the unconscious body of Yitzhak Yaacovy from the barricades and carried him off to Hadassah Hospital in Jerusalem, where he spent several months recovering from battle wounds.

From here, Yaacovy's career blossomed. He was invited to work on Prime Minister David Ben Gurion's staff, and there he met other young men — Teddy Kollek, who was to become mayor of Jerusalem, and Yitzhak Navon, who was to become President of Israel.

Yitzhak Yaacovy seems to us like a character out of Leon Uris's epic *Exodus*; he is a giant among men. His life seems almost too incredible to imagine, but it is true. You have only to read the list of battle wounded at Negba to find his name; you have only to shake hands with him and see the Auschwitz death-camp number tattooed on his forearm.

And this is the man who restored one of the holiest shrines of the Christian world. This is the man who gathered contractors and architects, religious scholars and engineers, historians and archaeologists, all together to rebuild the Street of Sorrow, with all the care for detail and religious sentiment they could find.

The first two Stations of the Cross are found within what was once the powerful Antonia Fortress, a massive bastion built by the evil King Herod and named in honor of his Roman mentor — Marcus Antonius (Mark Antony). The Roman garrison was stationed within the Antonia, and here also was the Praetorium, Pontius Pilate's judgment hall, and the prison where convicts were confined and tortured.

The Antonia was destroyed in A.D. 70 during the Roman destruction of Jerusalem. The street that led from its western gate was merely continued across the ruins of the fortress and out to St. Stephen's gate to the east. Through the centuries, various buildings were erected on either side of this street, and most remnants of the old Antonia were obliterated. Christian tradition, nevertheless, marked the site and kept its memory.

Today, there's a Muslim school — El-Omariye — on the south side of this street, and to the north there's a Franciscan compound with two chapels, a Bible school, museum, and library. Next to this is the Convent of the Sisters of Zion. The traditional site of the First Station, the Condemnation of Jesus, is located in the courtyard of the Muslim school, while a shrine and chapel commemorating the condemnation stands just a few yards away, across the street in the Franciscan compound.

The Chapel of the Condemnation memorializes Pilate's order that Jesus be scourged and crucified. The small chapel is always somber. A small stream of light filters in through stained-glass windows in its dome showing angels carrying the instruments of Jesus' torture. There are small statues depicting the meeting of Jesus and His mother along the Via Dolorosa. At the western end of the chapel, archaeologists have discovered Roman paving stones.

There is a plaque on the wall here. It says: " 'If any man would come after me, let him deny himself and take up his cross and follow me' (Mt 16:24). Jesus is searching for someone who will humble himself as He did and lovingly bear his cross. Will you be this disciple?"

We ask ourselves this question. Each must answer it in his or her own way. Even you, dear reader.

A few yards across the Franciscan compound, which is maintained in well-tended dignity with flowers and greenery garlanding remnants of Roman columns, is the Chapel of the Flagellation and the Second Station of the Cross. Tradition asserts that it was here that Jesus was scourged. Historians tell us that the common Roman practice was to whip condemned convicts with a "scorpion" before their execution. This type of whip was fitted with several barbed pieces of iron at the ends of its several lashes, so that these sharpened barbs tore and lacerated the victim's flesh, thus increasing the pain of execution.

The Chapel of the Flagellation is built in the medieval style of the Crusader period and was renovated in 1927. A crown of thorns is situated over the sanctuary. Of extraordinary interest are the three famous stained-glass windows by Cambellotti depicting the flagellation of Jesus, Pilate washing his hands, and the freeing of Barabbas. This small chapel also has an altar dedicated to St. Paul, who was also imprisoned in the Antonia Fortress.

A plaque on the wall says: "The Savior, scourged for our sake, covered with wounds, promises us: In My wounds there is power to heal all who are enslaved by the desires of the flesh. If you call upon My name, I will set you free."

Back out on the street, we face westward and see an arch spanning the Via Dolorosa. Tradition claims that it was here that Pilate's "*Ecce Homo*" mocked Jesus: ". . . Jesus came out, wearing the crown of thorns and the purple robe. Pilate said to them, 'Here is the man!' " (Jn 19:5).

Our pilgrimage along the Via Dolorosa has been focused at "traditional" sites. For many centuries, Christians simply believed that the traditional sites where they prayed along the Via Dolorosa were indeed the actual places of the Passion. They needed no proof. There were a few skeptics, certainly, who wouldn't believe that centuries of tradition could preserve the truth intact. But in the past century, by an unusual twist of events, the skeptics were proved wrong.

We make a short detour off the Via Dolorosa just past the Second Station and enter the Convent of the Sisters of Zion. This convent was built in 1857 by Father Alphonse Ratisbonne, a French Jew who converted to Catholicism. He chose this site because it abutted the Ecce Homo Arch, where tradition claimed Pilate had mocked Jesus. Archaeological studies, however, have proved this couldn't be. The arch, they say, was built in the year 135, a century after the Crucifixion. It had been part of a triple arched "Triumphal Gate" that the Roman Emperor Hadrian had erected as an entry to his new city of Aelia Capitolina, built upon the rubble of Jerusalem.

The skeptics had the first laugh. But then the archaeologists dug a little deeper. And in the basements of the convent, they discovered extraordinary remains of the ancient Antonia.

The Sisters of Zion accompany pilgrims visiting their convent and discuss the meanings of the numerous artifacts it contains. First, a stop by their small museum reveals several diagrams and models of Jerusalem and the Antonia Fortress during the days when Pilate represented imperial Rome here. There are also several interesting artifacts, such as the rounded stone missiles that were hurled at the Holy City by the Romans during the siege of Titus in A.D. 70. This museum, however, is but a preparation for a visit to the Lithostrotos.

Ancient texts describing the Antonia say that the western third of the mighty fortress consisted of a great parade ground where the Roman legionnaires would stand inspections, train, and also relax at games during their free hours. This parade ground was a paved square — or Lithostrotos — and here, within the protection of the fortress, Pilate would make his proclamations and also condemn his prisoners to death.

Archaeologists ferreting around in the basement of the convent have uncovered large sections of this Lithostrotos, as well as some of the foundations of the Antonia's massive walls, and thus have given proof to "traditions" held dear by century upon century of Christian heritage. The present-day Via Dolorosa is indeed found on the ancient route followed by Jesus during His Passion.

The nuns of the Sisters of Zion point to four different types of Roman paving stone the archaeologists have uncovered. One type is the simple flagstone — flat, unmarked, and the type upon which Roman soldiers marched and stood their inspections. A second type of stone is mostly flat, but has shallow channels cut into it. Such stones were used to direct rainwater down into cavernous cisterns, hollowed out of the bedrock beneath the Roman fortress, which can still be seen today.

A third type of paving stones has a series of parallel grooves cut into each block. Such stones are found along the path which horses would have traveled as they entered the western gate. The grooves apparently gave the paving stones better traction and helped to prevent horses from slipping on smooth pavement.

The fourth type of paving stone, however, is certainly the most interesting. Such stones have game markings scratched into them. There is much documentation that Roman soldiers enjoyed various games during their off-hours. Some games were simple gambling pastimes, with dice or "board-game" markings scratched into a stone pavement. Other games were a bit more violent, and one in particular, "Basilicus," could be quite malicious. *Basilicus* is taken from the Greek *basilikos* and means "royal." The victim of this game was given the "royal" treatment.

One cannot but recall the words of the Gospel: ". . . the soldiers led him away inside the palace (that is, the praetorium); and they called together the whole battalion [or cohort, about five hundred men]. And they clothed him in purple cloak]the color of royalty], and plaiting a crown of thorns they put it on him. And they began to salute him, 'Hail, King of the Jews!' And they struck his head with a reed, and spat upon him, and they knelt down in homage to him. And when they had mocked him, they stripped him of the purple cloak, and put his own clothes on him" (Mk 15:16-20).

Among the several game markings found carved into the paving stones of the Lithostrotos, in an inner part of the Antonia that was likely part of the praetorium, the archaeologists have found one stone which was used for the game "Basilicus." Was it here, upon these stones, that the Roman cohort tormented Jesus, mocked Him, and set upon His head the crown of thorns?

The western part of the convent is joined to the Ecce Homo Basilica (and, incidentally, *basilica* is derived from two words, *basilike oikia* or "royal house"), and in this church we find more remains of the Antonia Fortress, including two small rooms that sheltered the guards stationed at the bastion's gates. Jesus must have passed by these guardrooms as He left the Antonia on the way to Calvary.

We step back outside and turn right along the Via Dolorosa. Its cobbled pavement leads us westward, first up a small knoll and then down the opposite side. The street is bounded on both sides by edifices of stone, facing one another at a distance of only twenty feet or so. The Via Dolorosa is relatively narrow, and it is all one pavement. There is no sidewalk.

A few cars occasionally push through this part of the street, as do several donkey carts, Arab boys with pushcarts, and women who balance trays of fresh-baked rolls and breads upon their heads. A few shops line the street on the left side, catering mostly to pilgrims, who can purchase various religious articles, postcards, camera film, and related tourist items. Most of the buildings are residential, two-to-three-story stone houses with flat roofs and clotheslines extended from their balconies.

Jesus walked this way with His cross. Was this a mostly residential street at that time? Did the soldiers continue to torment Him while He carried the cross up this little knoll and down the other side? Did the crowd along this narrow street jeer Him? Were there some who stood in pity or compassion?

About a hundred yards down this sad street, we come to an intersection, and here the Via Dolorosa turns left and passes in front of a Polish Catholic chapel built by Free Polish soldiers during World War II. This is the Third Station — Jesus falls for the first time. An ancient pillar, set into the outside wall of the chapel, marks the precise site. Inside the chapel, the pilgrim finds two paintings of Jesus falling beneath the burden of the cross as well as a small Polish Catholic museum. A relief sculpture of Jesus stumbling beneath the cross is seen in an archway above the main door. Outside, the Via Dolorosa is paved with ancient Roman stones.

Across the street there is a small vegetable market and a little café where a few men are sitting at small steel tables outdoors and sipping cups of rich Turkish coffee. Farther down to the right is an Israeli health clinic, where an old man is standing on the steps. A woman and a little boy emerge from behind him, and the boy is sniveling. He cradles a bandaged left arm. The woman bends over and helps the child blow his nose into a tissue. They walk across the street, where the woman purchases an ice-cream stick from a vendor in front of the café and gives it to the boy. He stops sniveling.

Yes, there is life along the Via Dolorosa today.

After a dozen or so yards, the Via Dolorosa turns right, up a long hill. It is a fairly steep climb. Indeed, the paving of this part of the Street of Sorrow is done as a series of broad steps. The way also becomes more narrow, with only ten or twelve feet of space between the facing buildings. At the bottom of this hill, we come to the Fourth Station — Mary sees Jesus with the cross. The site is located in a small oratory next to the entrance of "Our Lady of the Spasm" Church, which is maintained by Armenian Catholics. In the crypt of this church is a sixth-century mosaic which, according to tradition, marks the precise spot where our Lady stood when she met Jesus along this Street of Sadness. Although the church is barely a century old, built in 1881, it stands on the site of an earlier Byzantine Church of St. Sophia.

What words are there, what prayers are there, that can express the profound emotions which must have been felt at this tragic meeting? There is an empty feeling by this Station, a helplessness, a great sadness. And for just a moment, our minds drift away from Jesus' Passion and think of the devastating shock which must have tormented the Blessed Virgin. Truly, this must have been the start of the most sorrowful hour of her life.

Farther upward the stepped street climbs, past a few small shops. The Via Dolorosa here is no more than an alley, and indeed a roof spans overhead, blocking out the sun. We are entering the ancient *shuks* of Jerusalem, the marketplace. We pass another small oratory marked with the Roman number V — Simon of Cyrene is forced to carry the cross.

Jesus must have been near exhaustion climbing this slope with the heavy cross laid upon His shoulders. The Gospels recall that "they [the Roman soldiers] compelled a passer-by, Simon of Cyrene, who was coming in from the country, the father of Alexander and Rufus; to carry his cross" (Mk 15:21).

Cyrene was the principal city of Cyrenaica, a Roman

province in North Africa, located where Libya is today. But Simon is a hellenized Hebrew name, so it's likely that the man who helped Jesus carry the cross was Jewish. But scholars generally agree that his two sons Alexander and Rufus had distinctly non-Hebrew names.

Many scholars think that Simon was probably a Jewish merchant who had returned to Jerusalem for the traditional Passover holiday and was merely an innocent bystander when the Romans conscripted him to work. The great significance of laboring with Jesus under the weight of the cross must have been tremendous for Simon, and some historians believe he soon became active with the Christian community in Jerusalem after the Crucifixion. Ancient sources also record the names of Simon's sons, Alexander and Rufus, as being active in the Christian community.

There is a slight indentation in the oratory's wall at the Fifth Station, and tour guides often tell their groups that this marks a spot where weary Jesus rested under the weight of the cross. It's a curious old notion, unsupported by any religious traditions or historical evidence. But pilgrims, nevertheless, are drawn to the spot and rest their own hands against the recess.

Jesus must have been truly suffering on this hill, for the Romans did not draft Simon of Cyrene as a gesture of mercy. It is more likely that they feared that Jesus would simply collapse and wouldn't be able to carry the cross to the top of Calvary otherwise.

Upward still, the Via Dolorosa follows a course through the darkened alley of the *shuks*. Several shops are lining the right and left sides of the narrow street. They sell souvenirs of interest to pilgrims and tourists, as well as some light snacks. And then we arrive at the Sixth Station of the Cross — Veronica wipes Jesus' face. This station is said to be the site of St. Veronica's home, where she, taking pity on the suffering Jesus, risked the hostility of Roman soldiers to wipe His face with her veil. Stories and traditions associated with Veronica's veil, which supposedly received the image of Jesus' face painted in sweat, dust, and blood, are well circulated through the Christian world and are often the subject of heated controversy.

The shrine at this Station is tended by the Greek Catholic "Little Sisters," and in the foundations of this building archaeologists have found what they presume to be the remains of the Crusader monastery of St. Cosmos. Did Veronica know Jesus? Was she a member of the early Christian community? Or did pure human compassion move her to ease the sufferings of one she thought to be a simple criminal condemned to death? Debates on these issues continue, and perhaps they'll never be resolved. It was a brief moment in history, a fleeting gesture of sympathy in the midst of tremendous agony. And therein lies the message of this Station. How many of us are reluctant to make even gestures of love and sympathy in this suffering world? How many of us feel our modest efforts are of no value in this world ruled by nuclear threats and hate?

Veronica's goodness was not in vain.

Farther still, we trudge upward along the stepped street until we reach an intersection at the top. There is a vegetable market here, and many people rush back and forth, haggling over the price of green peppers and scallions. Here is the Seventh Station. Here — Jesus falls for the second time.

Even with Simon helping, the weight of the cross must have been tremendous. And to this, modern archaeologists suspect that there might also have been a tremendous psychological shock, for here Jesus likely saw His own execution order.

Archaeological studies reveal that the ancient Gate of Judgment stood at the place where generations of Christians venerated the Seventh Station. The Gate of Judgment was the traditional exit from the city of Jerusalem for condemned convicts, and here their official execution orders were posted on the columns of the portico. Two Roman Catholic chapels are found at this station. Here we read a plaque recalling the Gospel of St. John: ". . . and he went out, bearing his own cross, to the place called the place of a skull, which is called in Hebrew Golgotha. . ." (19:17). This plaque also is inscribed with an additional comment: "Whoever belongs to Jesus must follow the path He took, for love is compelled to accompany Jesus on the Way of the Cross."

By the time Jesus had reached this gate leading out of the city, there was a large crowd following Him. But while He was mocked and tortured in the Antonia at the hands of the Romans, He found sympathy and sadness out in the streets of Jerusalem among the common Jews living there at the time.

Just beyond the Seventh Station, beyond the Gate of Judgment, once stood a small knoll. Today, of course, this knoll is incorporated within Jerusalem. Nevertheless, the pilgrim must still climb up an incline, on St. Francis Street, to reach the Eighth Station of the Cross. There is a Greek Orthodox monastery here, dedicated to St. Charalambos, and in its outside wall there is a cross that marks the site of this Station — Jesus speaks to the women of Jerusalem.

The Gospels tell us of the event: ". . . there followed him a great multitude of the people, and of women who bewailed and lamented him. But Jesus turning to them said, 'Daughters of Jerusalem, do not weep for me, but weep for yourselves and for your children. For behold, the days are coming when they will say, "Blessed are the barren, and the wombs that never bore, and the breasts that never gave suck!" Then they will begin to say to the mountains, "Fall on us"; and to the hills, "Cover us." For if they do this when the wood is green, what will happen when it is dry?' " (Lk 23:27-31).

It was here, on His way to Calvary, that Jesus warned of impending catastrophe — suffering that indeed would be so bitter that those without children were considered more fortunate. And surely, the people of Jerusalem did see mountains fall upon them.

The prophecy to the women of Jerusalem was realized in A.D. 70 when Titus Flavius Sabinus Vespasianus, son of the Roman Emperor Vespasian, led four full Roman legions, plus another five thousand Roman garrison soldiers, and an uncounted following of mercenaries, Syrian auxiliaries, and allied gangs against Jerusalem. They were determined to sup-

The Holy Land

press a Jewish revolt that had started four years earlier as a result of Emperor Nero's desecration of the Temple, the confiscation of lands, and the seizure of Jews for slave labor.

The mountains began to fall on Jerusalem when the Roman Tenth Legion set up their catapults on the Mount of Olives and began to shower boulders down into the Holy City. The siege of the city began in March. By July, the city had exhausted its stores of food. There followed starvation, disease, and constant attacks by the Romans. There was not even a place to bury the dead.

In the end, more than a million Jerusalemites died; the city was devastated, the Temple destroyed. The tragedy was immeasurable.

The Street of Sorrow is well washed with tears — surely for the sufferings of Jesus on the way to Calvary, but also for the knowledge of future human suffering. Along the Via Dolorosa one finds the afflictions and the compassions of the ages. It is as painful as our Lady's seeing her Son being led to execution. It is as loving as St. Veronica's soothing gesture. It is as profound as the Passion of the Messiah.

14 *Passus et Sepultus* •
Calvary and the Church of the Holy Sepulcher

WE STEP DOWN from the little rise where Jesus spoke to the women of Jerusalem and make a right turn down El-Attarin Street for a short walk down this busy market thoroughfare. It is jammed with pushcarts, pedestrians, and donkeys carrying their burdens. Shortly, however, broad steps rise off to our right. This is the beginning of the Hill of Golgotha — Calvary.

From here on, we are treading through the Church of the Holy Sepulcher. But this church is much more than a shrine sheltering the tomb where Jesus was laid to rest — the Holy Sepulcher. It is a sprawling complex of buildings, compounds, and little nooks where dozens of Christian communities vie with one another to keep a presence near the side of the Crucifixion and Resurrection of Jesus.

The Ninth Station of the Cross — Jesus falls for the third time — is located by an ancient column which forms part of a doorway into a Coptic Church. Off to one side, we can see clusters of little white huts which are actually built upon the roof of St. Helena's Chapel, part of the Church of the Holy Sepulcher. The huts are inhabited by Abyssinian monks. There is no room within the church itself for them to create a pemanent presence, and so they are content to live on the roof, just so that they can be perpetually close to the site of the Paschal Mystery.

We return back down the steps and back along El-Attarin Street for a few more steps before turning right again. To our right are several oriental shops, and a few of them deal in truly artistic religious objects. There are many beautiful sculptures and paintings, but most appealing are the several antiquities they offer — including some extraordinary icons. On the opposite side of the street is the Lutheran Church of the Redeemer.

Farther along, we see the old Crusader Muristan to our left, and straight ahead, the main entrance to the Church of the Holy Sepulcher. We enter into a courtyard area, all paved with blocks of limestone. We pass through great wooden doors, centuries old, and to our right rises a flight of stairs leading up to a broad platform.

The steps are steep, and at the top we are standing upon the site of Calvary, Golgotha, the Place of the Skull. Station Ten — Jesus is stripped of His garments — is located in the southern nave of the platform, and a mosaic pattern marks the site of this Station on the floor. A few steps away is the Eleventh Station — Jesus is nailed to the cross. There is a small and simple altar here, and a mural behind it depicting Jesus nailed to the cross. Both the Tenth and Eleventh Stations are on Catholic property, which is tended by the Franciscans.

Over on the opposite side of this small platform is the Twelfth Station — Jesus dies on the cross. The site is tended by the Greek Orthodox. There is a silver disc located under the Greek altar, and this marks the site where the cross was set into the ground. It is possible to reach through a hole in the center of this silver disc and actually touch the bedrock of Calvary.

I have known people who were skeptical over claims that these sites are actually the places where Jesus was crucified. They were skeptical until they visited. The atmosphere upon Calvary is still charged, still mystical, still permeated with agony and sacrifice and forgiveness and love. There are no words to describe the emotions and feelings upon Calvary. There are no words, dear reader, that I can offer you to describe the melancholy and grief of Calvary, nor the desolation of the Passion.

Feelings give way to thoughts. We stand upon Calvary and see very clearly its message. For here Jesus died as a man. Down below, at the Tomb, we may seek divinity and the Resurrection. But here, upon the rock of Calvary, we find only expressions of Jesus' humanity, we find only love and forgiveness. Was it not here, where Jesus was tormented and mocked, where soldiers gambled to win His clothing, and offered Him vinegar to quench His thirst, where He suffered terrible pain — was it not here, at the worst of times, that He said, " 'Father, forgive them; for they know not what they do' " (Lk 23:34)?

Can there be a greater expression of forgiveness? Can there be greater love?

It was here also that Jesus proved His own human weaknesses and cried to the heavens in the ancient Hebrew tongue — " '*Eli, Eli, lama sabachthani?*' that is, 'My God, my God, why hast thou forsaken me?' " (Mt 27:46) Jesus felt abandoned by the Father. He felt alone.

Is there a more human feeling than a sense of being deserted?

We stand upon Calvary and lose track of time. Is it ten minutes or two hours? Thoughts run rampant, riot in our minds. We see the flickering candles lit by pilgrims. And somewhere from the depths of memory comes the echo of Gospels heard over and over down through the years. It was here that the earth quaked and the rock of Calvary split, so that the veil of the Temple was torn and the centurion standing before a lifeless Jesus said: " 'Truly this was the Son of God!' " (Mt 27:54).

Nearby is the Thirteenth Station — Jesus' body is taken from the cross. It is marked by a simple Franciscan shrine, a carved wooden statue of our Lady. It is a reminder that Jesus' agony ended when He died upon the cross, but that the Blessed Mother's pain continued.

Down another steep flight of steps, we pass by a red, rectangular "Stone of the Anointing," marking the spot where, according to tradition, the body of Jesus was cleansed and anointed before being set in the tomb. The Fourteenth Station — Jesus is laid in the Holy Sepulcher — is but a few yards away. And, indeed, the Gospels confirm that the tomb was located near Calvary.

The Holy Sepulcher is a bizarre bit of architecture located directly beneath the great church's domed roof. The rock-cut tomb is completely covered by an aedicula — that is, a small shrine with the architecture of a building. Usually, this architecture is described as "grotesque" in the formal meaning of the word — that is, of unnatural shape, incorporating fantastic and incongruous figures. Many people think this aedicula is clearly inappropriate (even *ri*dicula) and are all for replacing it.

But it's what's inside that matters, for the aedicula is merely the covering over the tomb. We step through an ornate Victorian doorway and into the antechamber, the Angel's Chapel. There is a small pedestal in the center, and within it are fragments of the stone that was used to block the entrance to the tomb after Jesus had been laid within. Stooping through a low doorway, we enter the inner chamber of the tomb, the Holy Sepulcher itself. It is a small chamber, measuring about six by seven feet. Half of it is occupied by a white marble slab, where the Body of Christ rested between the Crucifixion and the Resurrection.

Today the tomb is shared as a shrine by the Armenian, Greek Orthodox, and Roman Catholic Churches. Many candles flicker within. Pilgrims file through the close tomb. They whisper brief prayers, touch their fingertips upon the white marble slab, and then depart. And all the while, a clergyman from one of the churches sharing the tomb keeps a vigil in the inner chamber.

It was here that the stone was found rolled back and the angel said: "Do not be amazed; you seek Jesus of Nazareth, who was crucified. He has risen, he is not here. . ." (Mk 16:6). It was here that the greatest event of all time occurred.

It was here that the great mystery of faith was accomplished, the mystery recalled every time someone proclaims, "Christ has died, Christ has risen, Christ will come again," or "Dying, you destroyed our death; rising, you restored our life. . ." or "Lord, by your cross and resurrection you have set us free. You are the Savior of the world."

Who remembers the ancient phrases? How many recall, from somewhere back in their childhood, the Latin: "*Crucifixus etiam pro nobis: sub Pontio Pilato passus et sepultus est. Et resurrexit tertia die secundum Scripturas*"?

It was here. It was here!

And still there are some "Doubting Thomases" around — although we cannot ask Jesus to appear before them, invite them to touch His wounds, and say, " 'Do not be faithless, but believing' " (Jn 20:27).

There are, however, several excellent scholars who are working in and around the Church of the Holy Sepulcher, and they are turning up some interesting facts and arguments. Rev. Dr. Jerome Murphy-O'Connor, O.P., is one of them. Speaking to the Israel Interfaith Association recently, the Dominican priest said that the site of Calvary and the Holy Sepulcher has been traced back to more than a century before the Crucifixion. Back in those pre-Roman days, the site was outside the north walls of Jerusalem and was being used as a quarry.

"There's been a church there since the time of Constantine," Father Murphy-O'Connor said. "The first buildings were started in 326, and the dedication was in 335. We have an eyewitness account of that. Eusebius, who was Bishop of Caesaria, was present and later wrote an account of the ceremony and a description of the building."

The Dominican said that there is no absolute certitude of facts that can confirm the site of Calvary and the Holy Sepulcher, but "in terms of probability, which is the best that can be hoped for when dealing with ancient texts or ancient sites, it's about as good as you can get. We're told by St. John that Christ was crucified outside the walls of the city. And according to Jewish custom, graves had to be outside the walls as well. Now, we know from previous archaeological excavations that the site of the Church of the Holy Sepulcher was outside the walls through the first third of the first century. It wasn't incorporated into the city until the building of the 'Third Wall' by Herod Agrippa in the year 41. That was about ten years after the Passion."

There are several reasons for believing the church marks the holy sites, the priest said, explaining that "when you have a quarry that was abandoned about 100 B.C., you have, outside the city, vertical surfaces of bedrock like the walls of a room. So then if you want to dig a burial cave you just go straight in. It's very simple. Otherwise you have to go down and in, a much more complicated process."

The Catholic scholar recalls that "St. John tells us that the Tomb was in a 'garden.' Well, in a region like this where you have sandstorms, any empty quarry is eventually going to end up with a certain amount of soil. Seeds are wind-blown, and then with a little rain we have in winter you soon have what passes for a garden in this part of the world. In that quarry also was a big block of stone left by the quarrymen. First of all because it was cracked, but also because it's very bad stone. It's very soft. You can almost rub it away with your finger. That became Golgotha."

The priest went on to explain: "The equivalent of beer cans and plastic bags were dumped into this abandoned quarry as well, especially in the site where the unfinished block of stone was, creating a rubbish dump. Now, the Romans didn't have in Palestine, at least not in Jerusalem, a regular place of execution. And certainly you would never have had Jewish tombs so close to a place of execution. So my theory, but again this is a very personal theory, is that when the Romans decided to execute Christ, they passed the judgment; then they said to the centurion on duty, 'Well, take him out and do it!' And since on this occasion the charge was that he was claiming to be 'king of the Jews,' this particular centurion thought it would be the greatest joke in the world to crucify him on what was effectively a rubbish dump."

Father Murphy-O'Connor is a professor of New Testament and inter-testamental literature at the Ecole Biblique et Archaeologique Francaise in Jerusalem, and his theories agree with Gospel descriptions. He believes that the Tomb was never before used, as the Gospels tell us — but he also thinks that it was intended only as a temporary resting place. Jesus was crucified on a Friday, and the disciples had to remove the Body from the cross and place it in a tomb before sunset, because of Jewish law. So they chose the nearest tomb as a temporary resting place. "This is, of course, why they went back after the Sabbath. I suspect the real reason was to move the body somewhere else . . . hence the big surprise."

Identification of the tomb's location was preserved — from the time of the Resurrection until the time of Emperor Constantine three hundred years later, according to the priest — by "word of mouth. Because what happened was that not only did you have that area brought within the city by Herod Agrippa, but then Hadrian flattened the ruins of Jerusalem to create Aelia Capitolina, and the area of the quarry he buried under a big platform on which he erected two buildings. One was a temple to Aphrodite; the other some sort of market-control building, a purely secular edifice. Hadrian chose that spot not, I think, to spite the Christians, but simply because if you look at the contour map you'll see that's a ridge right on the Cardo Maximus, the main street of Hadrian's city.

"Anyway," he continued, "the site of the tomb was known before Helena arrived, because Makarios, the Bishop of Jerusalem, had already been agitating for a church on that site. But it was only when Constantine sent his mother that money came. Of course, that's not a terribly strong argument. You have a Middle-Eastern bishop taking an old lady for a ride. But of course, walking along behind Helena were a whole squad of little-guys-in-dark-suits-carrying-briefcases, whose mission in life was to ensure that the Emperor's mother was *not* taken for a ride. So the minute they heard where the Tomb was located — under a big platform with two big buildings, all of which would have to be torn down, that they would have to build a church and reerect that commercial building somewhere else — money must have been a consideration. Particularly because right beside the site there was a big empty space: the Forum, with the triumphal arch which you now find in the Alexander Hospice.

"I think you'd have a rather naïve view of human nature if

you thought the financial men in the Empress Mother's entourage didn't sidle up to the bishop and say, 'Look, your Grace, uh, if you move it just fifty yards south — that's all we're looking for, just fifty yards, a hundred yards at the most — we'll make it worth your while.' And that's where the miracle comes in, of course. The bishop couldn't be bought!''

Constantine's church was damaged by the Persian invasions of 614, but restored by the Emperor Modestus in 640. It was torched by the Muslim Ikshhids in 934, and then burnt again by the Fatimites in 969. Then, in 1009, it was demolished by El Hakim Bir Amr Allah, the Fatimid Caliph of Egypt, who was intent upon spreading Islam by the sword.

"From what we know from the written record, Hakim left nothing," Father Murphy-O'Connor said. "There's a little trace at the back of the present aedicula in that little Coptic chapel: a bit of molding that's either from a previous monument or from the original rock tomb. But no one has ever excavated that, or surveyed it very thoroughly."

However, he noted, there are records of what Constantine's aedicula looked like, "the shell of rock-hewn burial chamber, partly embellished by masonry . . . represented in models which were brought back to Europe by early pilgrims. It is also represented on the 'Monza flasks,' the little silver pilgrim flasks that were also brought back in Europe in the sixth century. You put all the evidence together and you can reach a very accurate picture of what the aedicula in Constantine's church looked like, and it's absolutely nothing like the horrible edifice we have today."

Byzantine Emperor Michael IV negotiated the rebuilding of a chapel on the site in 1037, and eleven years later Constantine Monomach won further improvements from the Caliphs. But this all collapsed in 1077, when the Seljuk Turks pillaged the shrine. Persistent Muslim outrages at the Holy Sepulcher and other Christian shrines led Pope Urban II to preach the First Crusade at the Council of Clermont in 1095. Four years later, the Crusaders captured Jerusalem and went about rebuilding her shrines. A major undertaking was the nine-year rebuilding program for the Church of the Holy Sepulcher, and most of this Crusader building remains standing today. The Crusader kingdom lasted only until 1187, when Saladin drove them out and reestablished a Muslim caliphate.

The following centuries witnessed intermittent damages to the venerable church, some of which were considerable, such as the destruction that accompanied the Kharismian Tatar invasion of 1244. But as the centuries passed, Christian Europe gained strength while the Muslim lords ruling the Holy Land weakened. Thus, the Europeans were able to impose concessions — such as free access to Christian shrines, and their periodic repair.

A serious fire in 1808 caused much damage within the church, and two years later renovations included the construction of the present aedicula which covers the Holy Sepulcher. There is some discussion of removing the present structure and replacing it with something like the original aedicula built by Emperor Constantine. "It's a Victorian monstrosity," Father Murphy-O'Connor said in describing the present structure, "which is cheerfully described by some people as a 'hideous kiosk,' a not at all inaccurate description. Now it's even more urgent to take it down, if only because it's badly maintained and only held together by unsightly steel girders."

Repairs to the Church of the Holy Sepulcher are still in progress, although they're hampered principally because of the internal conflicts among the many communities sharing the building. Dan Rossing is an official with the Israeli Ministry of Religious Affairs, serves as a mediator between the communities, and often wins agreements through which vital repairs can be made without one Christian community infringing upon another's rights. At times, this can be a ticklish business — for example, when a single column is owned by two different churches, and is in need of repair. Even more difficult for the Israelis is mediating between the New York-based Russian Orthodox Church and the Moscow-based Russian Orthodox Church — both are claiming property rights dating back to the time of the tsars.

How does one make a decision? Follow King Solomon's lead and offer to cut the baby in half? The Israelis are naturally more sympathetic to the Americans. But a decision in favor of the American branch might offend the Moscow branch — and what implications might this have for the hundreds of thousands of Jews that the Soviet Union refuses to let emigrate? On the other hand, should the Israelis bend to Moscow's claims, there would be substantial internal unrest, because few Israelis are willing to snub America's friendship and goodwill.

Sometimes, it seems as if every stone in the church is disputed. But nevertheless, quite a few restoration programs have been completed in recent years, and the renovation of the great dome above the rotunda and the Holy Sepulcher itself is one of the major accomplishments.

All the while, however, the great church is in frequent use. And Easter services in particular are most appealing. Thousands of Catholics squeeze into the narrow route of the Via Dolorosa and the dark chambers of the Church of the Holy Sepulcher for the week-long ceremonies that draw people from around the world to Jerusalem.

The week of pageantry starts on the Friday before Palm Sunday, with a Solemn Mass on Calvary at eight o'clock in the morning in commemoration of the Seven Sorrows of the Blessed Virgin Mary. Later in the day there is a procession through the Church of the Holy Sepulcher. Again on the following day, there is Mass, plus processions and Solemn Office at the Holy Sepulcher. On Palm Sunday, there is the annual Blessing of Palms, followed by a procession, Pontifical Mass, and chanting of the Passion at the church. Then on Monday as well as Tuesday and Wednesday of Holy Week there are more processions, Masses, and pageantry.

On Holy Thursday, there is a Pontifical Chrism Mass with Blessing of the Oils at 7:00 A.M., and the doors of the Church of the Holy Sepulcher are then closed. Other ceremonies — Washing of the Feet and the Tenebrae Service — are conducted. There's a 7:00 A.M. Good Friday Mass on Calvary.

And at 10:15 A.M. the Franciscans lead the great Way-of-the-Cross procession along the Via Dolorosa to the Church of the Holy Sepulcher, where a Tenebrae Service is then conducted. Candles are extinguished, one by one, symbolic of the life ebbing from the body of Jesus. At seven o'clock in the evening, Catholics gather at the Church of the Holy Sepulcher for a Funeral Procession.

On Holy Saturday there is the Blessing of the Fire and of the Baptismal Font at the Church of the Holy Sepulcher, followed by a Pontifical Mass there, a procession, Solemn Compline, and a Pontifical Office.

At 6:30 A.M. on Easter Sunday, there's a Pontifical Mass at the Holy Sepulcher and a solemn procession led by the Roman Catholic Patriarch of Jerusalem. Later, there are more processions, and a Solemn Eucharistic Exposition. This recitation of ceremonies and processions, dear reader, is meant to relate that the Catholic presence at this most holy shrine is very much alive and active. Through the year, there is a daily Solemn Mass and a procession there. It is a vibrant and profoundly meaningful experience. Here, the Church thrives. True, the building is shared by dozens of Christian communities, but we have seen internal politics improved very much in recent years, and tremendously since Mark Twain wrote: "All sects of Christians (except Protestants) have chapels under the roof of the Church of the Holy Sepulcher, and each must keep to itself and not venture upon another's ground. It has been proven conclusively that they cannot worship together around the grave of the Savior of the world in peace."

Our visit to the Church of the Holy Sepulcher must also include a tour through the building's many chapels and shrines. The Holy Sepulcher itself stands in the center of a great rotunda at the western end of the building. Eighteen massive columns rise from the rotunda to support upper floors where there are chapels, meditation cells, and storage rooms, and above all this soars a great leaden dome.

The largest open area of the church is just east of the rotunda, known as The Katholikon. It's a Greek Orthodox cathedral. A stone chalice, dating from Crusader times, stands in the center of the floor and is located midway between the Holy Sepulcher and Calvary. Medieval maps marked this site as the center of the earth.

On the opposite side of the rotunda there's a dark, ancient, rock-cut Jewish tomb, which the Syrian Jacobites established as a chapel and in which they claim Joseph of Arimathea was eventually buried. North of the rotunda is a Catholic altar and shrine marking the traditional site where St. Mary Magdalene saw Jesus after the Resurrection (see Jn 20:1-18).

Beyond is the Franciscan Chapel of the Apparition, which commemorates Jesus' appearance to His mother. To the right is a sacristy where the spurs and swords of Godfrey de Bouillon — the Crusader king who captured Jerusalem in 1099 — may be seen. Nearby is a small altar which includes a fragment of a red Roman column, revered for sixteen centuries as the Column of the Flagellation.

Following through the northern end of the church, we pass the gloomy and soaring Seven Arches of the Virgin — remnants of the pre-Crusader church. On our left we pass by a Greek Orthodox chapel, "The Prison of Christ." And directly ahead is another Greek chapel, St. Longinus's Chapel, commemorating the Roman soldier who pierced Jesus' side with his spear (see Jn 19:34). Next is the Armenian Chapel of the "Division of the Raiment" commemorating the casting of lots of Roman soldiers for the clothing of Jesus.

A few steps farther on, a stone stairway descends to our left. Its walls are embellished with hundreds of crosses, perhaps thousands, carved by pilgrims who have visited over the centuries. At the foot of these steps is St. Helena's Chapel, also tended by the Armenians. Archaeologists believe that this chapel was a crypt in the original basilica built by Emperor Constantine. There are two altars, one dedicated to Constantine's mother, St. Helena, and the other to St. Dismas, the penitent thief who died on his cross beside Jesus.

More steps lead yet deeper into the earth, and at the foot we come to the Roman Catholic Chapel of the Finding of the

True Cross. This extremely important chapel had been lost for centuries, and only in 1965 did Franciscan archaeologists excavate through tons of rubble to find the remains of a large cistern dating from the Roman period. According to tradition, after the Crucifixion on Good Friday, Roman soldiers hastily tossed the crosses off Calvary, and they tumbled into an open cistern. In 326, St. Helena, in exploring the traditional site of Calvary, located the True Cross here.

Returning up the flights of steps, we turn left and continue through the church, past the Chapel of the Mocking where, according to tradition, Jesus rested for a moment during His Passion, and on to the Chapel of Adam. This small chapel marks the traditional burial place of Adam, and it is located right at the northeast base of Calvary. An ancient fissure runs up through the rock of Calvary, linking the site where the cross of Jesus was set to the place where the first man was buried. Tradition also says that on Good Friday some of the Blood of Jesus ran down along this fissure, touched the skull of Adam, and restored it to life for an instant.

Opposite this, at the northwestern corner of Calvary, are the tombs of Godfrey de Bouillon and Baldwin I, the first two Crusader kings of Jerusalem, respectively. The pair were brothers. In 1099, Godfrey was one of the commanders of the Crusaders, and with Baldwin at his side he successfully drove the Muslim defenders from Jerusalem. His victorious rule was brief, and he died only a year later. But Baldwin then took his brother's command and established the Crusader kingdom with firm supply links from Jerusalem to the coast of Jaffa, and then across the Mediterranean to Europe.

A number of convents, monasteries, and chapels are built as wings to the Church of the Holy Sepulcher, and here one may walk through a spectrum of Christian faith. We stroll through St. Abraham's, the Greek Orthodox Convent, and then St. John's Armenian Chapel, followed by St. Michael's Ethiopian Chapel. Across the courtyard is St. James's Greek Orthodox Chapel, followed by St. John's with its beautiful Byzantine and medieval baptistry, and then the Chapel of the

The Holy Land

Forty Martyrs. There's the Altar to the Three Marys, another Armenian Chapel, and an Egyptian Coptic Chapel. Near the great Crusader doors is the Roman Catholic oratory of Our Lady of Sorrows, where Mass is celebrated daily; it is a splendid, light, and clean chapel — much in contrast to the gloom of the rest of the church. Beneath it is the Greek oratory of St. Mary of Egypt.

There is such a bewildering diversity of Christianity here, and one wonders how they will ever be reunited. Can the spirit of ecumenism heal this fragmentation? And if so, how should it be healed? Perhaps the Copts might be brought to recognize the authority of the Holy See. But to what extent should their ancient traditions, language, and liturgy be reformed? I am only a layman, but the difficulties posed by these divisions seem very formidable to me.

We discuss these perplexities outside the church door with Yakub Nusseibeh, an eighty-two-year-old Muslim who is the official opener of the doors to the Church of the Holy Sepulcher. Yakub's family had been given the keys to the church in 1187, when Saladin finally drove the Crusaders from Jerusalem and declared that the keys for the church should forever be kept in Muslim hands. Back around 1830, the Ottoman Sultan took the keys from the Nusseibeh family and entrusted them to another Muslim family, the Joudehs, although the Nusseibehs remained the legal openers of the doors.

"It is going in that direction [toward unity]," Yakub admits. "There is less hostility among Christians today. They are learning to get along with one another. If they keep at it, they may solve their differences. It takes goodwill and time."

Yakub knows about goodwill. In 1985, he was honored as a Distinguished Citizen of Jerusalem for his decades of work to promote understanding and goodwill among Jerusalem's Arab and Jewish populations. He has labored on behalf of the Red Cross and the U.N. Relief and Works Agency, as a guide around holy sites, as an educational adviser, and a translator.

"*Hic Iacet Philippus de Aubingni. Cuius Anima Requiescat in Pace. Amen*," reads the old gentleman as he studies a Latin inscription in the church's courtyard. "It means, 'Here lies Philippe d'Aubingni. May his soul rest in peace. Amen.'

"Sir Philippe was one of the Crusaders, but a peaceful Crusader," Yakub recalls, almost as if he had been there himself. "That was during the Sixth Crusade, after Saladin had regained control of Jerusalem. The Crusaders then came to negotiate a truce with the Muslims, and also to negotiate access to Christian holy places, and this was granted. You see, it is possible for even Muslims and Christians to settle differences peacefully. So I think Christians *and* Christians should be able to do this, too.

"Sir Philippe was one of the signers of the Magna Carta in England, and he was a tutor of King Henry III when he was a boy," Yakub goes on. "He was an educated man, concerned with legal rights, and concerned with peace. With men like this, we can solve many of the world's problems."

Yakub Hassin Nusseibeh died shortly after talking with us. He passed away on January 25, 1986. And the world is diminished, for he too was an educated man, concerned with legal rights and concerned with peace. He practiced his family's ancient occupation of opening the doors to the Church of the Holy Sepulcher. He also practiced another occupation — opening the doors to wisdom, tolerance, and peace.

But then, aren't these among the reasons for having a Church of the Holy Sepulcher? Aren't these the ideas Jesus preached and died for?

15 *Ascendit in Caelum* •
The Ascension and the Heritage

JESUS APPEARED several times after the Resurrection. St. Matthew (28:9-10) tells us that Jesus greeted the women who came on Easter Sunday to visit the Holy Sepulcher. St. Luke (24:13-35) tells us that later, on that first Easter, Jesus appeared on the road to Emmaus, walking with two disciples and lecturing them on the need for the Messiah to have suffered. There is a lovely, bucolic sanctuary at Emmaus today, located about seven miles northwest of Jerusalem. It is still possible to walk upon the Roman paving stones there and, as Jesus was, to be invited to join the Franciscan community living there and break bread with them.

St. John (see 20:19-29) tells us of yet another appearance, on the night of Easter Sunday, when Jesus joined the disciples in a locked room: "Jesus . . . said to them, 'Peace be with you.' When he had said this, he showed them his hands and his side." Eight days later, St. John tells us, Jesus appeared again and invited the Apostle Thomas, who was not at the previous appearance, to touch His wounds: " 'Have you believed because you have seen me? Blessed are those who have not seen and yet believe' " (see Jn 20:24-29).

St. Matthew (see 28:16-20) tells us that Jesus appeared to the disciples on a mountaintop in the Galilee, where He told them: " 'All authority in heaven and on earth has been given to me. Go therefore and make disciples of all nations, baptizing them in the name of the Father and of the Son and of the Holy Spirit, teaching them to observe all that I have commanded you; And lo, I am with you always, to the close of the age.' " St. John (see 21:1-23) reports yet another appearance along the shores of the Sea of Galilee.

The book of the Acts of the Apostles tells us that, through

the forty days after the Resurrection, Jesus made repeated appearances to His disciples, continuing to teach them about the kingdom of God, and that on the fortieth day, after instructing them to carry the Gospel "to the end of the earth, . . . as they were looking on, he was lifted up, and a cloud took him out of their sight" (see Acts 1:1-10).

This was the Ascension. If we climb to the peak of the Mount of Olives, we find several different shrines that claim to mark the site of the Ascension. They are all within a few hundred yards of one another, and they reflect religious chauvinism more than historical accuracy.

The site accepted by most Christians, including Catholics, is today a Muslim shrine. The Byzantines originally built a shrine here, but it was destroyed by the Persians. The Byzantines returned for a short while and rebuilt the shrine, and this was later embellished by the Crusaders. It is a rather small, octagonal building with a domed roof covering the Rock of Ascension — the last place where the feet of Jesus touched this earth.

With the Arab conquests, the shrine was converted to Muslim use and remains so to this day, for the Muslims venerate Jesus as a prophet, an equal with Moses, David, and the other Old Testament personalities.

Still, it seems unreasonable that the site of the Ascension should be a Muslim shrine.

We look westward across the landscape and see Jerusalem in all its glory. The dominant landmark we see is the great Dome of the Rock — another Muslim shrine. And this, too, seems unreasonable.

The Dome of the Rock stands on Temple Mount — the site of Solomon's Temple. For Jews, this is the most sacred land on earth, the very center of their religious heritage. Some Jewish Zealots have tried to demolish the Muslim shrine with explosives, but fortunately they were captured, tried, and imprisoned. Such destruction would have led to even more bloodshed in an already mourning Middle East.

Although Temple Mount is identified by most people as a

primary Jewish heritage, there is also much Christian attachment.

Remember, it was in that Temple that Jesus taught and debated with the Pharisees, establishing much of the Church's doctrine.

The Muslim claim is somewhat weaker. Jerusalem isn't mentioned in the Koran — not even once. According to Muslim tradition, Muhammed ascended into heaven from Moriah, the great rock beneath the golden dome. It's a picturesque tradition, but it has difficulty standing up to historical reality.

Historical fact: Muhammed died in A.D. 632.

Historical fact: In A.D. 632, Jerusalem was still very much a part of the very Christian Byzantine Empire. The Holy City did not fall to the Arab armies until A.D. 637 — five years after Muhammed had died.

There are other contradictions, and as systematic archaeological explorations continue, many of these contradictions will be resolved.

An important motivation behind this book is to demonstrate that such modern exploration is confirming Christian traditions of centuries. The Gospels tell us that Jesus preached in a synagogue in Capernaum (Capharnaum). In recent years, Franciscan friars excavated that ancient town and found that synagogue. And so they have probed in other places where the Gospels have told them Jesus conducted His ministry — in Nazareth and Jerusalem and Cana and many other towns — and they've been finding just what they expected.

There is a certain comfort in knowing one's faith can stand up to this sort of scrutiny. Christians can rest assured that modern scholarship is not developing any inconsistancies such as the one between Muhammed's historical death and the earliest possible date a Muslim could have entered Jerusalem.

All this scholarship is also illuminating the Gospels, making them more meaningful. Until the recent discovery of the Dead Sea Scrolls, when the world learned that the Essenic sect called itself the "sons of light," Christians had little understanding of Jesus' reference to the "sons of light" in the Gospel according to St. Luke.

And all the other recent discoveries point us in the same direction: there is tremendous historical accuracy to the Gospels.